P9-DHF-247

DARKNESS TO LIGHT

DARKNESS TO LIGHT

A MEMOIR

LAMAR ODOM

AND CHRIS PALMER

BenBella Books, Inc.
Dallas, TX

Copyright © 2019 by Nunnbetter Productions

BenBella

BenBella Books, Inc.
10440 N. Central Expressway, Suite 800
Dallas, TX 75231
www.benbellabooks.com
Send feedback to feedback@benbellabooks.com

Printed in the United States of America
10 9 8 7 6 5 4 3 2 1

Library of Congress Cataloging-in-Publication Control Number: 2019002815
ISBN 9781948836081
ISBN 9781948836203 (ebook)

Editing by Joe Rhatigan
Copyediting by Scott Calamar
Proofreading by Laura Cherkas and Lisa Story
Text design and composition by Aaron Edmiston
Cover design by Sarah Avinger
Cover image by Scott Hebert
Printed by Lake Book Manufacturing

Distributed to the trade by Two Rivers Distribution, an Ingram brand
www.tworiversdistribution.com

Special discounts for bulk sales (minimum of 25 copies) are available.
Please contact bulkorders@benbellabooks.com.

To Cathy, Mildred, Liza, Destiny, and Lamar Jr.
—L.O.

To my parents, Ransford and Sally
—C.P.

This is where I was born.

This is where she died.

I can close my eyes and still see it.

It's cold outside. There are no leaves on the trees.

The concrete is cracked and broken.

Cathy has to take the bus.

She doesn't know where Joe is.

The bedroom is empty.

I am alone.

I am Lamar Joseph Odom.

And I am alive.

I was born in the autumn of her twenty-third year. She had always wanted a child. A boy who would grow to be handsome and tall. When she got pregnant, she was living with her mother in an upstairs bedroom and working for the New York City Department of Transportation in Queens.

Joseph Odom was a charismatic Vietnam War vet who worked as a janitor in the Woodside Houses projects in Queens. My mother was visiting a friend there when Joe first noticed her and won her over with his good looks and an easy brand of charm. She liked his smile; he liked her round, pretty eyes. He was twenty-three. She was twenty-one and just finding her way in the world.

Shortly after their first encounter, Cathy Mercer, tall, lithe, and beautiful, was walking by Woodside when Joe saw her again. He was cutting the grass, and his boots were stained green. He shut off the mower and met her at the sidewalk.

"What's up, Slim?" he said. That's what he would call her. A cute nickname to break the ice and set him apart from the other guys.

"Nothing, just trying to get home," Cathy replied. "But I don't have a token." She needed to jump on the 7 train. Joe had but one subway token in his pocket. He needed it to get home.

"Take mine," he said. He reached in his pocket and placed the token in her palm. Cathy smiled and gave him her number.

"You gonna call me, right?" she asked.

"I got the number memorized."

My father walked the seventy-two blocks home. He repeated her phone number the whole way. That token, something so small yet quintessentially New York, is the beginning of my story.

Joe grew up in Williamsburg, Brooklyn, long before the hipsters invaded.

"We was on the block," my dad told me, years later. "We had to do for ourselves. It wasn't pretty like it is now. We had drugs and temptation. We were young and innocent. Our lives were at stake."

My dad first tasted marijuana at fourteen. From there he dove headfirst into hard drugs. He hustled on the block. He dealt to pimps, gangsters, and bangers. He'd get a fix from a neighborhood dealer with the promise of more to come if he could sell on the street.

He often found himself holed up in an abandoned building getting high. His parents were furious when he dropped out of high school his sophomore year. When Joe finally told his father, he ordered Joe into the family car, a 1968 Cadillac Eldorado. They drove for two hours, talking about repercussions and dreams and where Joe's life was headed.

Back in the driveway, my grandfather put the car in park. They sat in silence for ten minutes. He looked at Joe and saw himself in the youngest of his five children. This boy, who was bright and tall and strong, began to cry.

"I'm a drug addict," Joe said.

"I know, son," said his father.

The next day my dad enlisted in the army. There was a recruitment office near their apartment. Two weeks later he was shipped to Fort Dix in New Jersey to begin his military training. Shortly after, he was deployed to Saigon. He reached the rank of E-4 Specialist and trained with M16s.

The experiences in a foreign land traumatized him.

He returned to Brooklyn a broken man. He was introduced to heroin in Vietnam. Many soldiers used it to deal with the stress of taking human life. It was how they coped. They were made to kill people they didn't know. They pulled the triggers and stood there as the bodies dropped. It destroyed my father psychologically. Any empathy he had evaporated.

Joe moved back into his parents' apartment. He was twenty-two and paranoid, depressed, anxious, and without direction. He looked over his shoulder on the rare occasions he left the apartment. And he only left in search of a fix. Within the year, Joe contacted a Veterans Affairs administrator who had one arm and an addiction of his own. He helped my father get back on his feet. That's how Joe got the job at the Woodside Houses.

Cathy and Joe didn't know each other very well, and in many ways, they never would. But Joe said they would give birth to a prince.

The things a man will tell a woman.

So, love blossomed in the ghetto. Concrete gave way to something softer. Joe loved her. Cathy would tell her friends about this guy from Woodside. She wanted a husband and a son and a home. They had started something that could not be undone. Their lives would take disparate paths, but ones that would forever be bound by me . . . the only thing they truly had in common.

I weighed seven pounds, fourteen ounces when I came into the world. "Man, he is long," said Joe at St. John's Hospital just past noon on the first Tuesday of November. "And he looks just like me. We done good, babe."

I would be at once precious and tormented. Cherished and forgotten.

My grandmother Mildred Mercer was born to a family of sharecroppers and former slaves in rural Athens, Georgia, in 1934. When she was in her twenties, after scraping together twenty-nine dollars for a seat on the Greyhound, where she was relegated to the back of the bus with no air-conditioning, she and her sister moved to a tough working-class neighborhood in the Bronx in search of jobs and with designs on settling down and starting families of their own.

When Mildred had her first daughter, Cathy Celestine Mercer, they moved to a modest two-bedroom house on 131st Street and Linden Boulevard in South Ozone Park, Queens, just north of John F. Kennedy International Airport. My grandparents plopped down $250 for the down payment. The small abode was Queens through and through with its black gate and awning-covered porch, which was fronted by a row of tidy bushes. Their neighbors were bus drivers and toll workers and street sweepers and clerks in local government offices. They had found their heaven in the middle of New York's biggest and most Italian borough.

I grew up in Grandma Mildred's house, and it was always the center of neighborhood activity on 131st Street. Whenever there was a major life milestone or tragedy, our family and close neighbors gathered at the house. Graduations, birthdays, wakes, and new jobs were all reasons to get together over a barbecue in the backyard to either celebrate or commiserate.

My grandmother was the matriarch, setting house rules and curfews, and making certain that bellies were always full of her turkey wings, cabbage, fried chicken, and dumplings. I lived in this house growing up, except for a short time right after Joe and Cathy got married.

It was 1985, and I was six years old. And for the brief time Joe and Cathy were married, we lived in an apartment near the beach in Far Rockaway, Queens. I was part of a complete family.

But the tranquility and good times were short-lived. I have to search deep in my mind to find happy moments from my childhood. And I still have to convince myself that they actually happened. The only memories that come forth easily involve fear, pain, and anxiety. The smell of Mildred's meals starts to fade and my mother's angelic smile blurs in my memory. All that's left is a frightened, powerless ten-year-old boy.

2

I took less than a year for my parents' arguments to grow louder and more frequent—setting off a period of angst, uncertainty, and turmoil that would shape my life indelibly. That's when the violence started. Even though I couldn't understand the source of the arguments and why my parents just couldn't get along, I knew what it felt like to see my father hit my mother. Her screams and then muffled cries made me feel powerless as I hid from my father's anger.

It scared me. What's worse, it scarred me. I'm still recovering from the trauma of being unable to protect my mother from the noise, from the pain, from the arguments. And one day, my mother screamed "Enough!"

And in a flash, my father was gone, leaving behind his seven-year-old son. Less than a year after my parents married, my father returned to the streets where to me he became as much a rumor as a mystery. He loved my mother once. Very deeply. A long time ago when my eyes were young. But he left, and my heart filled with hate. And yet I wanted him to love me more than I hated him. He always had the benefit of the doubt . . . his weakness more powerful than my greatest strength.

My hate for him burned. But I sought his junkie approval above all things.

Mom and I moved back into Grandma Mildred's house on 131st Street. Along with my mother's sister, JaNean, we tried to salvage our family and insulate ourselves from the harshness of everyday life. I shared an upstairs bedroom with Mom. It was the first door on the left and had been my mother's alone before I was born. She moved another twin bed in and cleared out some closet space. Each and every night we talked to each other until one of us fell asleep. I always seemed to fall asleep first.

Soon she got a new job as a corrections officer at Rikers Island, one of the most notorious prisons in America . . . where there was no assurance its staff would make it home after they clocked in. Most people assumed that because she had such a dangerous job, she was some tough-as-nails broad. But she wasn't. Now, she didn't take any mess from anyone, but she wasn't hardened. That place couldn't rob her of being a mother or a daughter. Her humanity was more resilient than the concrete walls and razor wire that housed hopelessness and despair.

In my young eyes, she was soft and angelic. Beautiful. Her delicate voice a song on the wind. Even at five feet nine she never seemed imposing to me. More of a protector who would rather love than quarrel. And all her love was for her little Mookah. That's what she called me.

Once we settled in at Grandma Mildred's house, my life started to return to some semblance of normalcy. The sounds of my mother's favorite artists, Anita Baker and El DeBarge, filled the house. She sang along to Anita's "Giving You the Best That I Got" as Grandma Mildred fried chicken in the kitchen on a Saturday night.

This was the best time of my young life. My mother was happy. I felt safe. I was a regular kid.

In 1991, I turned twelve and made the Lynvet Jets, a youth football squad for eleven- to fourteen-year-olds. My mother came to nearly every game she could when she wasn't working. During one of our Saturday afternoon games, while playing quarterback (I dubbed myself a young Randall Cunningham), I rolled out to the right and got hit pretty hard by a much bigger kid.

As I writhed on the ground, the only thing worse than the pain in my knee was my complete embarrassment as Mom dashed onto the field to take care of her only son.

"Ma, what are you doing?" I screamed as my teammates laughed.

At Christmastime, presents under the tree were sparse. Birthdays usually yielded just as little. Sometimes it was a piece of athletic equipment or a Nintendo cartridge, but it didn't matter because I knew she tried. One particular Christmas I kind of wish she hadn't. She worked extra shifts at Rikers for a month to get me a new, fancy mountain bike with rugged tires and racing stripes. The only problem was that it had these weird, old-timey U-shaped handlebars. When I rode it down the street, I had to awkwardly steer it as my knees popped up to my shoulders while pedaling. It was way too hard to look cool on it in the hood, so I parked it behind the house and hoped my mother wouldn't notice I had stopped riding it.

I was seven when I first dribbled a basketball at P.S. 155, an elementary school that was a block away if you hung a right out of my front gate. Little kids gathered there after school and on weekends to thrash around the asphalt imitating basketball gods such as Rod Strickland, Mark Jackson, or Pearl Washington, heaving the ball toward the rim with both hands.

As I hit middle school, I turned my sights toward Lincoln Park, the neighborhood proving ground where physicality and artistry clashed on a daily basis. The park had an unforgiving asphalt court with rims with no nets in the shadow of the Van Wyck Expressway. It's where everything went down, and you had to bring it or go home. It didn't hurt that by eighth grade I had sprouted to six feet even. I always played with guys who were older, quicker, and stronger than me. When I was thirteen, I told them I was fifteen so they'd let me in games. The running joke in my neighborhood was when I would actually tell the truth about my age, someone would say, "Damn, you've been fifteen for two years."

My game developed rapidly during the educationally brutal runs at Lincoln Park. I insisted I was Magic Johnson reborn. I loved the way the six-foot-nine point guard could bring a crowd to its feet with the flip of a no-look pass and how his teammates loved to play with someone who could get the ball to them in just about any situation. I discovered early on that while my mind wandered in the classroom or during a test, I could figure things out easily on a basketball court.

I became a problem solver. Where other kids forced shots up, I drew defenders and made the extra pass. I saw the value in surveying the entire concrete court to make plays instead of pounding the ball into the pavement with my head down. I wasn't exactly bucket-getter Bernard King, but I was unusually tall for my age and not without skills . . . to the point where the local tournament announcers began to invite me to play at Lincoln Park.

Around this time I'd see my father about once a month. He'd stop by to give me some money or maybe a pair of shoes. I still had a tremendous amount of animosity toward him. The gulf between us was flooded with unanswered questions: *Why did you leave us? Why did you hit my mother? Why did you choose drugs? Why did you try to destroy our home? Why didn't you love me?*

I was just a fucking kid.

I imagine those conversations were just as hard for him as they were for me. But *he* was the adult. *He* ran and hid and refused to deal with things, leaving me to fall deeper down the hole of confusion and regret. Accountability was a concept that never occurred to him. Getting high was easier. He thought he could just show up and press twenty dollars in my hand and everything would be okay. I didn't know it at the time, but he was handing me a blueprint to follow, and the things I hated him for . . . I would become.

3

The only thing I knew about cancer when I was a kid was that you could die from it. Adults always explained cancer away as God's will. I never had to meet it face-to-face and didn't know it could touch the ones closest to me. Until it did. I was too young to feel anything when my dad's father died from it about six years before my mother got sick in the summer of 1991. I remember my mother slowing down and not laughing as much. She had a cough that wouldn't go away, and her energy decreased more and more by the month.

After a stay in the hospital for exhaustion, the doctors gave us the words we dreaded. "Cathy, you have colon cancer."

I didn't even know where on the body that was. I thought my mother would get better even if things might not be the same. I tried to do everything I could to make her feel happy while deeply burying my own fears. I thought that if I could make her laugh it would ease her pain, but I never knew how much pain she was in because she hid it from me.

Eventually, she stopped going to work. The physical demands and stress of her job at Rikers were far too much to bear. She began to have difficulty using the bathroom and climbing the stairs. Her appetite diminished almost to the point of nothing, and she had trouble digesting the food she did manage to eat. With my mother's reality becoming bleak, Dad began showing up to help out around the house.

By April 1992, she could no longer be cared for at home and was admitted to St. John's Hospital's cancer ward. There she continued to wither away, like she was disappearing right in front of me . . . literally being erased from my life.

The thing that hurt the most was that she was barely able to speak. Her beautiful voice had been stolen from her, and she could only offer a whisper. It didn't sound like Cathy; it was as if I were speaking to a stranger.

In the last few days of her life, I visited her nearly every day, and she tried to talk to me as much as she could. I could tell it was important for her. Sometimes she just whispered my childhood nickname over and over: "Mookah . . . Mookah . . . Mookah." She did her best to muster every last bit of strength from her tired body.

One day near the end I was sitting on her hospital bed as she clutched my hand. It startled me because her grip was tighter than it had been in a while. She opened her eyes halfway and spoke. "Be nice to everyone, Mookah."

My aunt and I got up and left the room so she could rest. I would never hear my mother speak again.

"She might be gone before we get home," said Aunt JaNean, after talking with the doctors.

We drove home in silence. I could see the world pass by outside the car window. It was silent and cold to me. I felt so small and alone. I was afraid. What would I do? Where would I go? When we got home the phone rang as we climbed the stairs to the front door. Grandma Mildred rushed to answer it.

She sat down in the kitchen, talking quietly. She hung up the phone. I stood in the doorway, looking at her with a blank face. "She's gone," Grandma said quietly. She began to pray.

I went upstairs, numb to everything around me, and sat on my bed. I picked up my basketball and left the house without anyone knowing. I sprinted up 131st, dribbling the whole way, the ball an extension of my hands. I got to the court and began to shoot. I took each shot desperately, as if each release of the basketball would somehow hold back the wave of pain and sadness that was heading my way.

I took shot after shot. The ball left my hand and floated, hanging there as if time didn't matter, before falling through the rim. The same hand my mother had held for the last time just hours before. Another shot. Then another. I'd been there for an hour when word began to circulate through the neighborhood that Miss Cathy had gone away.

Then a strange thing happened. Slowly, people began showing up at the court. At first, they just watched. They were classmates, neighbors, and old hoopers who had never even spoken to me before. Then they began to join in one by one, most never speaking so much as a single word. There were hugs and embraces, but few words. I could feel everything they never said.

We got you. We are here with you, Mookah.

My mother's funeral was a blur. I stared at the floor the entire time. I tried to block out the low sobs that cascaded from the first pew to the back row. I had been to funerals before where people were wailing and falling to their knees because a loved one had been taken too soon by the anger of the streets or the unforgiving finality of an anonymous bullet. But no one cried out at Mom's funeral. No one asked God why. Except me, although I dared not say it out loud.

Death was a cage for me, but it was a release for my mother. It was simply God's will. I guess didn't need an adult to tell me that.

We got you. We are here with you, Mookah.

The neighborhood had my back. Queens had my back. For the first time in my life, basketball had saved me. I could feel it lift me off the ground.

If only for a moment.

4

My mother was gone, but so was I. It felt like I had disappeared from my own life. I couldn't get her out of my mind. Every time the phone rang or the front door opened, I thought it was her. I couldn't sleep. I forgot the taste of the foods I loved. I couldn't remember the sound of my voice. It had been so long since I heard my own laughter. It felt like all of my emotions were just stuck, frozen in a time I longed to escape. I couldn't move. The world began to pass me by.

There's only one way I made it through: that damn basketball. I went to Lincoln Park nearly every day for two years. I poured every bit of energy I had into basketball, whether it was a pickup game, an organized tournament, or one-on-one. My handle became second nature as there was rarely a moment that worn-out basketball wasn't in my hands. I crashed the boards with abandon, using my height and leaping ability to smash opposing players' shots into the fence. I was determined to beat people off the dribble as if my life depended on it. And in truth, maybe it did.

My court vision, which would ultimately become the key to my game, began to sharpen. I could see passing angles even most adults couldn't. I thrived when it came to setting up my teammates. Touch passes, crosscourt finds, no looks. Every type of behind-the-back setup. I was getting pretty good, but I loved to play with the New York flash like the ballplayers who came up on these streets before me. To me it just felt like the natural thing to do.

And, not least important, by the time I was fourteen, I had grown to be six two, just one inch shorter than my father. I was ready for the next level: New York City high school basketball. I told myself that's where I would make my name.

In the fall of 1993, I enrolled at Christ the King Regional High School in Queens, about ten miles from my house. I was thirteen and ready to make new friends and leave my pain as far behind me as I could. Even though I was an average student and didn't care for structure or homework, high school seemed as good an adventure as any.

CTK had a multicultural student body with a strong academic standing, and as a member of its thirty-first incoming freshman class, my grandmother liked the idea of me being surrounded by academically inclined students. Its basketball team was a powerhouse in the best high school basketball league in the country: New York City's Catholic High School Athletic Association (CHSAA).

Students were assigned to homerooms alphabetically by last name. That was my first stroke of luck. I didn't know it, but that policy would ultimately affect me for the rest of my life.

The school day started at 8:15 AM with a twenty-minute homeroom, which was just an excuse for my friends and me to clown each other. Nothing was off-limits: the outfit you wore two days in a row, personal hygiene, or whether you were in dire need of a shape-up. Well, that's what happened when I didn't show up late, anyway. I almost always showed up late.

But during that very first homeroom, I sat down in the middle of the classroom several rows over from a pretty Puerto Rican girl named Liza Morales. She looked away when I made eye contact. I flashed a little smile, and she returned it with an embarrassed grin. I knew I had to talk to her. Maybe I was going to like high school after all. The teacher was jabbering on about some important announcement, but I already had my head in the clouds.

One morning, before homeroom, I was standing at my locker, running late as usual, brushing my teeth.

"Why are you brushing your teeth in the hallway?" Liza asked me. "Don't you have a home?"

"You know I gotta be fresh for the ladies."

"Oh, please."

I started flirting with her. She always rolled her eyes, which I took as a sign she was interested. She never shut me down completely, and she punctuated her quips with a cute little laugh. I really didn't like going to school, but she gave me a reason to show up.

"You talk to too many girls," she would say. "Why you always talking to those chicken heads?"

"Don't worry about them. We were meant to be together."

But the truth was, we were complete opposites. She was always early. I moved like I didn't own a watch. Her locker was as neat as could be. Mine looked like a proving ground for tornadoes. Her grades and attendance were perfect. I rarely did homework, and I was absent so often my existence was merely a rumor. She wasn't into sports, ran with a totally different crowd, and thought I was only interested in one thing. Well, I was interested in that, but the truth is, no matter how different we were, I really liked her.

So, I started going to homeroom on time. Every day I sat one desk closer to her. I'd throw balled-up pieces of paper at her to get her attention. But when I did, she'd turn to look at me, and I had no idea what to do next. What could I say? I was fourteen, and I had never talked to anyone the way I wanted to talk to Liza.

Liza grew up in Woodhaven and took the Q11 bus up Woodhaven Boulevard and transferred to the Q54 to get to school. I'd usually get on the Q54 a few stops before her. I'd sit in the back of the bus trying to sneak looks at her, maybe get a smile and think of something funny to say by the time we got to homeroom.

I loved the ladies and they loved me, which is probably why Liza kept her distance. It was a little too much for her, being a good Catholic girl and all. Though sometimes I would gently take her hand and say with a flirty smile, "When are we going to hang out?"

"When you stop running around with all those other girls," she'd reply.

"I'm waiting for you and you alone."

She smiled.

High school had gotten off to a great start, but basketball try-outs couldn't come fast enough. Even though my mom wasn't there to offer her usual encouragement, I told myself that every-thing I did on the court would be for her. I made the freshman team, and after some strong games, the head coach, Bob Oliva, moved me up to varsity. Even though I felt I could compete, I didn't get a ton of run because the team was just so stacked.

There was a skinny freshman from the rugged Farragut Houses projects in Fort Greene, Brooklyn, named Erick Bar-kley, who I knew from the neighborhood. He was lightning quick and had the kind of maturity on the basketball court that college coaches were already starting to notice. Once he scored forty-eight on the future NBA star Stephon Marbury, who'd go on to win Mr. New York Basketball my freshman season. But Steph did give him forty-four in return. Oh, I forgot to mention that this epic showdown happened when Erick was nine and Steph was eleven. As an only child, I was always fascinated that Erick was the youngest of nine children. I think that's one reason why I gravitated toward him.

Erick was getting recruitment letters from St. John's and was a tough cover for anyone. We'd play one-on-one before and after practice and just throw everything we had at each other. Going against Erick, even more so than the games I played, helped develop my ability to dribble against pressure and get shots off against tough defenders. It was a crash course in becoming a tough New York City guard and I was only fourteen.

Then there was sophomore Speedy Claxton, a blur of a point guard from Hempstead who even might have been faster than Erick. And much like Erick, Speedy was from a large family of seven brothers and sisters. The team was so tight that Erick moved in with Speedy's family during his senior year.

We all were just family. That Christ the King team my freshman year included three future NBA players in Speedy, Erick, and me. But we were still kids. Speedy and Erick were both more accomplished than I was, and it wouldn't be until the following season that the course of my life and career would change drastically.

5

I n 1994, the summer between my freshman and sophomore years, I had the great fortune of sprouting seven inches. Now, not only was I six nine, but my coordination and agility had no problem keeping up with my height. Being at Christ the King was great for my visibility, but I was still very much an unknown prospect. Over the summer my game began to blossom exponentially, largely due to playing in the Riverside Hawks Amateur Athletic Union (AAU) program, which assembled some of the best AAU teams of all time, with several of its alumni going on to success in the NBA.

I started playing with Riverside that summer, which is when I first met a rambunctious, six-foot-six, do-it-all wing from Queensbridge named Ron Artest. His energy and effort on the court were like nothing I'd ever seen. He could handle the ball, shoot, and play the finesse game all while running you over like a bulldozer. His mood could fluctuate wildly, but we all just thought he was wild by nature.

One of the best big men in the country, Elton Brand, a soft-spoken, pensive six-foot-ten behemoth, anchored the middle. Oh, and we also had Erick Barkley to run the point. We would go around to all the big-time tournaments in New York and steamroll the other teams. If Erick didn't have the ball, it was in my hands. I'd push it up the floor and direct traffic and dazzle the crowd with an array of passes.

That's when my profile started to rise locally, and I first began to get comparisons to Magic Johnson. Recruitment letters started trickling in from local colleges like Hofstra, Manhattan, and Fordham. Other AAU coaches also picked up on my emerging talent and became interested in my services.

My sophomore season at Christ the King started out on a high note, especially on the defensive end. I was just erasing people's shots. In an early season game in December, I recorded seven blocks. One for each inch I had grown over the summer.

By January, I was fully blossoming on the basketball court, averaging fifteen points, eleven rebounds, six assists, and four blocks. I was more than halfway to breaking Christ the King's record for blocks in a season with ninety-five. We were 11–1 and climbing up the CHSAA rankings.

That same month we played Bishop Ford in their gym in Brooklyn. It's a game that stands out in my mind because it was one of the first times that I felt truly unguardable. I got into the lane with ease. I beat double teams with my dribble and the pass. It felt like I was flying on the break. The stands were packed, and I felt like a star. I notched my first triple-double, something that would become a staple of my career, with seventeen points, fourteen rebounds, and ten assists. Ford had Trevor Diggs, who was one of the best players in the city and would go on to play at UNLV. He put forty on us, but after the game all eyes were on me.

The opposing coach came up to me and shook my hand but didn't say a word. I had left him speechless! I didn't know it, but two people in the stands that night would affect the course of my career and life for the next few years. Gary Charles was one of the biggest AAU coaches in the country. His team, the Long Island Panthers, was one of the first dominant AAU programs on the East Coast. If you played for the Panthers, you were legit.

Gary was there to scout me, and he brought along one of his players, his de facto right-hand man, a five-foot-ten junior point guard from Queens named Greg Nunn. They called him the General.

"This kid is a monster," said Greg. "How are we gonna get him?"

"Don't worry about it," replied Gary. "I have a plan."

"But he plays for Riverside. They don't just let players get away that easily."

"His grandmother wants him to play for a black coach."

Gary always knew little bits of inside information like that. Having your ear to the street is what makes an AAU coach successful. He knew every angle, every hustle. Riverside put bomb-squad rosters together every year. The team that I played for was no joke. Riverside's head coach, Ernie Lorch, was old and white. Gary was young and black. That was Gary's play.

After the mobs of newfound fans began to scatter, I saw Gary and Greg standing on the court. Gary was precise and

to the point. He wanted me to play for the Panthers next summer. He introduced me to Greg. We exchanged a quick dap
and nods of respect. No hugs or flattery . . . just a very quick
New York greeting. I gave Gary my grandmother's number so
he could make his pitch to her, and I kept in touch with them
during the school year.

Meanwhile, Christ the King had unfinished business to
attend to. By the time the playoffs rolled around, we were a
sterling 22–3 and one of the top-five ranked teams in New York
City. On March 14, 1995, we headed to St. John's University
for the Catholic High School Athletic Association's semifinal. I
had nineteen points in a closely fought game against Harlem's
Rice High School. We won 70–61.

Four days later at Fordham University, we faced Bronx
powerhouse St. Raymond High School for Boys for the title.
We were amped up. Maybe a little too much. We were over-
aggressive, fouling unnecessarily. We turned the ball over and
couldn't seem to do much of anything. By the end of the first
quarter they were up 22–6.

Then we settled down and I took over. I made play after
play, setting people up for corner threes or swooping to my left
to finish at the basket with thunderous lefty dunks. I blocked
shots into the stands. Every time I touched the ball, the spectators moved closer to the edge of their seats. The roar of the
crowd gave me strength. In the end, I would make New York
City basketball history by setting the CHSAA record for points
in a championship game, breaking the mark held by Power
Memorial's Lew Alcindor (who would later change his name
to Kareem Abdul-Jabbar). I was named tournament MVP

and finished with a game-high thirty-six points along with ten rebounds, five blocks, and four assists.

I became a star. I was on the covers of newspapers. Girls began to flock in herds. The guys from Big Willies, a local club, even invited me to party there, despite the fact I was five years away from being legally able to drink. Grandma Mildred's phone wouldn't stop ringing. College coaches I had seen for years on TV came to my games and tournaments.

I thought about the cold nights at Lincoln Park. I thought about what it would be like to shake NBA commissioner David Stern's hand on draft night. I was somewhere in between the memory and the dream, but I was on my way toward fulfilling the dream.

6

Several months after my initial meeting with Gary Charles, the Panthers met at Foster Laurie, a Police Athletic League gym in Queens. When I walked in, somebody shouted, "Damn, Gary got it done! He got Lamar!"

Playing for the Panthers would be my first taste of the bitter sneaker war brewing between Nike and Adidas as they fought for players, teams, territory, and pretty much global domination. Both Christ the King and Riverside were sponsored by Nike, so naturally I just wore my Air Jordan 8s to my first Panthers practice.

"Nah, you ain't playing in them," Gary said as he handed me an Adidas shoebox.

After warming up, I felt pretty good about my decision to play for the Panthers. Going into the summer before my junior year, I was ranked as one of the top-five high school players in the city, along with three other future NBAers: Elton Brand, Tim Thomas, and Ron Artest. Gary felt that if he could find another top-ranked player at any position, the Panthers could have a shot at winning every tournament they entered, including the granddaddy of the summer, the Adidas Big Time Tournament in Las Vegas, which included sixty-four teams.

That player was Khalid El-Amin from Minnesota. Fast and strong, he proved why he was the number-one-ranked point guard in the country every time he stepped on the floor. I felt like we could win a national championship with me and Khalid alone.

I also started to develop a natural chemistry with Greg Nunn, a less heralded but Queens-hardened point guard who always seemed to find me in my sweet spots and picked up my game and natural tendencies really quickly. He didn't shoot much, but we complemented each other's games in a nice way.

Greg and I bonded off the court as well. When the Panthers went on road trips and stayed at hotels, we usually slept four to a room, but Gary always assigned Greg and me our own room. I didn't mind because with four guys crammed into a tiny hotel room, sleep and privacy were hard to come by.

Early that summer, we were at a tournament in New Jersey, and when we got back to our room after a game, Greg asked, "What's the deal with you? You're always so nonchalant and laid-back. You can't be this relaxed about everything. On the court you're a killer, but off it, you don't seem to care about anything."

"That's just how I am, I guess. I try not to worry about too much."

Actually, I had never really thought about how checked out I seemed. I thought at the time it was a body language thing. I was never loud or the center of attention; I simply liked being in the background. I moved at my own pace, but apart from being late for school or the occasional practice, no one had ever really said anything to me about my relaxed demeanor. I haven't changed much since then, but today I am more aware that behind that young teenager who just rolled with the flow was someone not entirely present.

As the summer of 1995 dipped into June, the Panthers headed to California to play in the Pump-n-Run Tournament at Long Beach State, where I held my own against top West Coast ballers like Paul Pierce, Schea Cotton, and Jason and Jarron Collins. A week later, we were back in New York and prepping for a tournament in Chester, Pennsylvania, which, in retrospect, illustrates just how much unsupervised freedom we had as teenagers.

At the time, Gary was only thirty-five, so he had a life of his own with plenty of obligations. With nearly every coach from the Big East and ACC at the Chester tournament, we couldn't miss it, but Gary had to go to his girlfriend's graduation and couldn't make the trip. He would meet us there later on. It wouldn't be a good look for the Panthers or any of the guys on the team if we didn't show.

So, Gary had Greg, the most responsible member of the team, drive us to the tournament. Did I mention Greg was sixteen with only a learner's permit? Gary put him in charge of driving me and eleven other high school players across three states. Gary organized a fifteen-passenger van, and we all piled in and made the chaotic 165-mile drive from Long Island, where Gary lived, to Chester. We laughed, joked, and made a ton of noise. No seat belts in a van swerving all over the road. Greg needed laser-like focus under dark and foggy conditions just to keep the van from careening into a guardrail.

We arrived late in the night, exhausted and starving. Of course, all the restaurants in town were closed. Half of us forgot IDs and some didn't even bring basketball shoes. Not to mention, no one had any money.

The next day we had to be at the gym at 8:30 AM for a 9:00 game. That meant we had to be up and getting ready at least an hour before tip-off. No one even thought to arrange for a wake-up call. What do you think happened? Greg got up late and frantically knocked on doors, trying to get everyone in gear. The problem was that he didn't know half the rooms the guys were staying in. We were still at the hotel at nine.

By some miracle, we all piled in the van and got to the game by the middle of the second quarter. They'd started the game on time and the Madison Broncos, a powerhouse team in their own right, were up 17–0. Tournament organizers had started the clock and for every minute we were late, they gave the Broncos a point. The Broncos were just shooting around on one end of the floor. We walked into the gym disheveled, and all these future hall-of-fame college coaches stared at us in disbelief. UMass head coach John Calipari couldn't help but laugh.

We hit the floor with Greg as our coach and went on a tear. In six minutes of the second quarter, we mopped the floor with the Broncos. I think they were so stunned they forgot their plays. By halftime the game was tied at twenty-four.

Gary showed up just then and didn't know whether to laugh or cry. He couldn't be that mad at us because the whole weekend was his doing. He was just glad we were alive. We ended up winning by nineteen.

John Paul Vincent "Sonny" Vaccaro wanted to be a running back. At five feet eight with broad shoulders and a curly Italian afro, his bowling-ball-like style seemed perfect for the gridirons of 1950s western Pennsylvania. But after blowing out his knee, he enrolled at Youngstown State and began organizing local amateur basketball events.

In 1965, he founded the Dapper Dan Roundball Classic, which was an annual spring exhibition game featuring twenty-four of the best high school players in America. This gave top coaches from around the country an opportunity to evaluate players. It was a radical idea, but the game would run for forty-three years and change the course of the sport. Basically, Sonny invented the high school all-star game. Through his street-smart brand of ingenuity, his charming gift of gab, and an uncanny ability to gain trust and see the big picture, he created what would become the system of modern amateur basketball and everything (good, bad, and ugly) that came with it.

It was his idea to sign basketball players to endorse major sneaker brands. In 1984, Sonny signed twenty-one-year-old Michael Jordan to be the face of Nike, forever changing sports marketing. That same year, he founded the Academic Betterment and Career Development (ABCD) Camp, a weeklong summer showcase for the best players in the country. After getting fired by Nike in 1991, Sonny took his camp to Adidas and vowed to challenge Nike for domination of the high school basketball world. Sonny Vaccaro became known as the godfather of high school basketball, and his impact on amateur basketball will forever be felt.

He was basketball's biggest power broker because he invented power brokering. Getting an endorsement from Sonny was like being touched on the shoulder by a great king. It was the seal of approval. He wasn't just *the man* . . . he could make *you* the man. He could shift the landscape of a high school or college basketball program with a phone call.

If there was one man to know, it was him. And one man who knew him was Coach Gary. Because of Gary's ability to land the top players in the country, Sonny sponsored the Panthers, providing the team with $15,000 worth of shoes and clothing and arranging for the Panthers to travel the country. The trade-off was that Gary would steer players toward Adidas-related events. And the ultimate endgame was to win the loyalty of top high school athletes, so if they made it to the next level, they did so wearing Adidas gear.

When I agreed to play for the Panthers, Sonny nearly threw his back out jumping for joy. In the next three years, there would be few players Sonny and his beloved wife of thirty-seven years, Pam, spent more time around than me.

To be invited to ABCD Camp meant you were the cream of the crop. So that's how, in July 1995, I found myself in the tiny brick gym on the campus of Fairleigh Dickinson in New Jersey for Sonny's annual showcase.

That summer produced one of the most talented groups of players in recent memory. There was Kobe Bryant, the consensus overall number-one player in the country. Vince Carter was a high-flying small forward from Daytona. Jermaine O'Neal was a six-foot-ten center from a small town in South Carolina and considered the best big man in the country. Rounding out the top was Tim Thomas, a do-it-all six-foot-nine senior forward out of Paterson Catholic in New Jersey. He had just come off a junior season with an average twenty-five points and fourteen rebounds per game. Out of any of the top players at the camp, Tim's game most resembled mine. Of course, I thought I was better than him, despite the fact he was a year older than me.

The competition that year was incredibly fierce. Everybody was out to prove they were the top dog. Rankings were always up for grabs, and every player wanted that "No. 1" next to his name. Kobe walked around like he owned the place. He shaved his head bald back then as a tribute to his hero Michael Jordan, and there was always a confident smirk on his face and a little extra swag in his step. Kobe had come from such a different background than I had, and we barely had anything in common, but I liked him right away.

On the first day of camp, things got heated quickly. Thomas and O'Neal were matched up in the last game of the day, and a buzz reverberated through the gym. Even the campers gathered courtside along with the coaches to see the first big matchup of the week. Tim liked to talk big on the floor and carried himself with a certain kind of edge. He wore New Jersey on his sleeve.

Jermaine didn't know what was about to hit him, but I did, because I had history with Tim. The previous summer, when I was as hungry as I was naïve, I had matched up against Tim at a tournament in New York City.

I lined up to guard him as he brought the ball up the floor. There were ten seconds left in the game, and I steeled myself while staring at Tim as he controlled his dribble. I was not going to get embarrassed.

"Young fella, how do you want this?" asked Tim. "You want a dunk or a three in your face?"

"Shut the fuck up!" I countered, partly because I was so surprised by his audacity.

"I warned you, young buck."

With that, he raised up and shot a three directly over my head that splashed into the rim at the buzzer. "It ain't your time yet," he said coldly as he walked off the floor, leaving me standing there. I was pissed, but what could I do? It was Tim Thomas.

Against Jermaine at ABCD, Tim came out firing the same way. He drilled a three in the game's opening moments right in O'Neal's face. "Bang!" Thomas shouted at Jermaine. "All day. That's for you."

"Ooh!" the onlookers said in unison with an almost hushed tone.

Jermaine, who was a soft-spoken please-and-thank-you kind of guy, had made his first mistake. He didn't respond. From then on Tim thought he was weak. He was all over him. The next trip down the floor Tim caught the ball in a triple-threat position, offered up a couple jab steps, and when O'Neal bit, he put the ball on the deck and pulled up for a jumper that ripped the nets.

"That's cash! That's cash!" said Tim, backpedaling down the floor.

After Jermaine responded with a couple inside buckets of his own, Tim caught a pass at the foul line while trailing on a break. He took one dribble, drop stepped, and threw down a nasty tomahawk dunk right on Jermaine's head. The gym exploded.

"You my down-south bitch!" shouted Tim directly at Jermaine. "My down-south bitch!"

It was as dominant a performance as I have ever seen of one top-ten player against another on the summer circuit and certainly one of the most embarrassing. But Tim pretty much coasted the rest of the week, leaving the race for camp MVP wide open. Kobe didn't mind, as he easily won the honor.

I got overlooked a bit at ABCD, but my stock was still high as I finished as one of the top-twenty players in the camp. Maybe Tim was right. It wasn't my time just yet, but there was a lot of summer left.

After ABCD, it was off to Las Vegas for the Adidas Big Time Tournament. Another brainchild of Sonny's. Of course, all the big stars came out—Tim Thomas and Kobe Bryant among them. Based off his showing at ABCD, Kobe was ranked the overall consensus number-one player in the country heading into his senior year. When Kobe moved from one court to another during camp or a tournament, dozens of college coaches would pick up their chairs and move right along with him. In other words, wherever sixteen-year-old Kobe was, that's where the action would be as well. And that's where you'd find Sonny.

In order to see everything, Sonny put Kobe's team on the court next to the Panthers, and the games would be lined with a who's who of amateur basketball. Duke's Mike Krzyzewski studied Kobe intently. Syracuse's Jim Boeheim did his best to make eye contact with me. Connecticut's Jim Calhoun and Florida's Billy Donovan jostled for the best sight lines all while making nice with top AAU coaches to try to get a feel for which way their star players were leaning with regard to their college decisions.

During the day in the hot gym, it was all business, but at night it was on. Remember what I said about lack of supervision? There wasn't a group of parents who made the trip with the Panthers to watch over us like what happens today. It was just a bunch of sixteen-year-old kids from New York who were used to being on their own from dawn till dusk. There's no way Gary could keep his eye on us, plus, he had a ton of meetings . . . usually some sneaker executive wining and dining him. Sonny was shaping him to be the next big power broker, and there were always deals to tend to.

Oh, and another thing. We didn't have to worry about social media. There was no Twitter or Instagram. The iPhone wouldn't be invented for twelve years, so people weren't walking around with a camera in their hand trying to score a viral video. Today, if a player leaves his hotel room, there's a good chance he'll end up somewhere on social media, but back then, luckily, that didn't exist.

One night, early in our Vegas trip, we decided to go out and hit the Strip. It was like nothing we'd ever seen before. I mean, we had been to Times Square in Manhattan, but that didn't compare. The flashing neon lights were hypnotic. There were fountains springing up from in front of five-star hotels. It just felt like opportunity was in the air all around us. But mostly, there were women. We weren't old enough to gamble but that hardly mattered. We wanted women.

So, we got a bright idea: let's buy some pussy. I had a few hundred dollars in my pocket that Gary had given me for this trip, and it was itching to be spent. So, Kobe, Greg, Tony Lee (a guard from Boston), and I headed out to the Strip. There were mostly young white girls walking up and down the Strip, and because none of us had ever been with a white girl, we pretty much had our mission for the night.

Since we were black and mostly over six feet six, we told every girl who would listen that we were in the NBA. But Kobe was a little bit different from us. He came from the pristine sub-urbs of Philadelphia's wealthy Main Line neighborhood and wasn't quite as street-smart as a bunch of kids from Queens. He was pragmatic and careful. He would think things out and worry about the consequences. He was always so aware. We just did things without thinking. Halfway through our pursuit, Kobe wasn't feeling it and decided to go back to his room.

"I'm just gonna roll back with Kobe," said Tony.

"Man, you better roll with us," I said. "You're gonna miss out."

Immediately, Greg and I picked up a couple girls without having to dig in our pockets. Our NBA story worked. Tony would have been much better off rolling with us, because next thing you know, Kobe's got a pretty young girl on his arm and peels out, leaving Tony standing in the dust by himself. We still laugh about that today. Greg and I stayed up all night, but the Panthers still managed to make it to the semifinals the next day.

When the summer AAU circuit ended, everybody went their separate ways. Since Greg lived close to me, we wound up hanging out for the rest of the summer. He lived in Far Rock-away with his mother, fifteen minutes away on the other side of Kennedy Airport in the Five Towns. If we weren't play-ing ball at Lincoln Park, our agenda was very simple: video games, weed, girls . . . preferably at the same time. But since we couldn't bring girls back to either one of our houses—and smoking at home was completely out—we always ended up at an older friend of Greg's, far from any kind of supervision.

By this time, Greg and I were hanging out pretty regularly. When we weren't at school, practice, or a game, we were usu-ally at one of our homes getting something to eat. No one in my family owned a car, but it hardly mattered because I didn't have a driver's license. So Greg would often borrow his mom's beat-up money-green 1994 Mazda MX-6 coupe. We'd cram four basket-ball players in that tiny little car. I'm six feet ten, but we made it work. It beat riding the bus, but it was always an adventure since there was usually weed in the car and Greg still only had a permit.

Back then, it seemed like everyone we knew smoked mari-juana. It was just a normal thing in the neighborhood. I always had access to it and being the most recognizable high school basketball player in the city didn't hurt. There was always somebody offering me some. I've never paid for weed in my life. But that's as far as we took it. Hard drugs were frowned upon. It wasn't cool, and we never touched anything stronger than weed from small-time pushers.

As the summer wore on, and I didn't have a tournament or a big game to prepare for, Grandma Mildred worried about me more than usual. Throughout my teenage years, I stayed out of trouble and wasn't into mischief or running with the wrong crowd, but with my mom dead and dad who knows where, my grandmother was all I had. The only real stabilizing force in my life. And I think she felt that way about me, too. I still hadn't opened up to anyone about how devastated my mom's death left me. I didn't talk about my depression or anxiety—hell, I didn't even have those words in my vocabulary yet. I was consumed with fear and panicked whenever I thought about losing another family member and being left alone.

Without a ball in my hand, I was consumed by loneliness. To deal with it, I isolated myself. I'd go into my room, close the door, and make myself cry. I thought that if I cried enough, I could make the pain go away. I would drain it from my body. But it never worked. I only felt more helpless. Being in the house made me sad. Seeing Mom's clothes hanging in her closet that she would never wear again. The mirror she looked into to get ready for work. The pots she used to cook from. Everything that reminded me of her was still and gathering dust. Every time I turned the corner a small part of me hoped I'd hear her voice calling me. But I never did. I had to get away from the things that reminded me of her.

And it was easy to get away. All I had to do was say I had a game or practice. Even if I didn't.

"Coach needs to see me, Grandma."

And just like that I'd be gone. I would try to come and go as I pleased while Grandma Mildred did her best to rein me in. If I came home at three in the morning, I wasn't allowed to go out the next night. She always hugged me the next day, but I knew she felt she was losing her grip on me. Junior year couldn't start fast enough for the both of us.

hadn't seen much of Liza over the summer, and she had assumed I was caught up in becoming a basketball star and the trappings of budding celebrity.

After clinching the CHSAA championship and winning MVP, as well as completing a productive summer circuit, I was on the brink of becoming the biggest high school basketball star in New York City. My stock was soaring, recruiters came calling at all hours, and the attention I received from women increased tenfold. And it wasn't just girls at school or on the train. I'm talking about women like the kind you see in clubs or on the block who would roll with the shot callers. I was six feet ten, so they thought I was a grown man even though I was only sixteen. I loved it.

But to be perfectly honest, I still thought about Liza. She knew me before any of this basketball stuff, and that endeared her to me. We hadn't gone on a date yet or even kissed, but I decided I wanted to step up my game with her. No more silly flirting. I needed her to take me seriously. So, one night, instead of doing my homework, I stayed up for hours writing her a love letter. I had never written one before and my handwriting was barely legible, but I needed to let her know how I felt. By the time I was done, there were way too many crossed-out words, and the paper looked like a wrinkled shirt exhumed from the back of my closet.

It didn't matter because everything I needed to say was right there above those blue lines on a single piece of loose-leaf paper. I folded it carefully and tucked it in my jacket pocket for safekeeping. Around one in the morning, I reached for the light to switch it off, but I stopped. I felt paralyzed. My mother's bed lay empty just a couple feet from mine. Her jewelry, dusty and untouched, lay on the dresser. I said a prayer. Not to God, but to Cathy. Maybe Cathy would hear me this time. I wanted to tell her about a girl.

The next day at school I missed homeroom, so I handed the letter to Liza before her sixth-period study hall.

"What's this?" she asked.

"Just read it," I said before quickly disappearing down the hallway.

She could tell I was a little bit shy when it came to being romantic, but I think it endeared me to her. She read the letter out loud to her friends and was flattered. She really got a kick out of it. A mutual friend of ours in that same study hall told her that one of my boys and I had made a ranking of the cutest girls in school, and that I gave her the highest grade.

Later that day, I saw her in the hallway. I had waited three hours to find out what she thought. She approached and smiled. She reached in her purse and handed me a piece of paper with her phone number on it.

My letter worked.

We started talking on the phone almost every night. Back then, all we had were landlines with just one number. Inevitably Grandma or Aunt JaNean would pick up the receiver somewhere else in the house and I'd have to yell, "I'm on the phone!"

About two weeks later, Liza and I went on our first date. We decided to see the movie *Independence Day* and doubled with another couple to keep things light. At the concession stand, I loaded up my pockets with candy, and then we settled in our seats as the house lights went low.

In the lobby afterward, I finished a Blow Pop lollipop and then fashioned the stick into a ring, which I put on Liza's finger.

"You know you're going to be my wife one day," I said.

Her eyes widened as she looked at me, her lips pursed with a brand of skepticism that could only come from a woman from Queens who had heard it all. Them Queens girls. They're just thorns without the rose. But not this one. Her gentle features softened and we paused for a moment.

There in the lobby, I kissed her for the first time.

After an exhausting but exhilarating summer on the basketball court, I was excited to suit up again for my junior year at Christ the King. We opened the season with a rematch against St. Raymond's. We returned almost our entire team, and this time it wasn't close. Erick Barkley went to the hole like a bolt of lightning. Forward Ira Miller caught fire from deep. We blew them out 107–78 in front of a sold-out gym. I had the best game of my career with twenty-eight points, sixteen rebounds, eight assists, and four blocks and was named MVP of the tournament.

"They just gave us a good, old-fashioned . . . how do I put this politely? Beating," St. Ray's coach, Gary Decesare, told the New York *Daily News* afterward.

We steamrolled through the 1995–96 regular season, finishing 25–0 as the nation's second-ranked team behind my seventeen points and ten rebounds per game. We were ready to defend our CHSAA title. The *New York Times* called me a "one-man wrecking crew" as we beat St. Raymond's yet again in the quarterfinals, as I went off for sixteen points, twenty-one rebounds, six blocks, and five assists.

Next up in the semis, we advanced to the title game after dispatching St. Francis Prep 68–46. We were giddy with the idea of an undefeated season. There was talk of us being the best New York City high school team in a decade. But it wasn't to be. In the finals, Rice High School jumped out to a 12–2 lead before we snapped out of our funk and tied the game at thirty-three by the half. I struggled to get good shots, and Rice's ball movement and hustle were more than we could handle. In the end, it was close. Rice's Bevon Robin drove the length of the floor and hit a crazy shot off the backboard with 1.3 seconds left in overtime to win it.

I was crestfallen. I sat on the bench and buried my head in my hands. I felt like I had let the team down. We had gone an outstanding 48–3 in the last two years, but I only thought about one thing: returning to the title game for the third year in a row and taking back what was ours.

I would not get that chance.

8

One of the most interesting people I've ever met on my basketball journey is Ron William Artest Jr., my mercurial, bruising, small forward of a friend. I've always gotten along great with Ron, but if you're familiar with his controversial NBA career, you'll understand when I say that sometimes it's been difficult to figure him out.

A complex mix of emotions, energy, and angst wrapped around a big heart, Ron appeared to be this large, tough guy who wore Queensbridge on his sleeve and people conveniently overlooked his softer side. People talked about his rage while looking past his empathy. They thought his scowl on the basketball court defined him, but it was his sympathy and loyalty for others that made him who he was and still is to this day. Like I said, he's complicated.

A year or so after I left Riverside and started playing for the Panthers, we competed in the vaunted Wheelchair Classic at Riverbank State Park on the Upper West Side in Manhattan. After the tournament, as we were leaving, Ron rolled up on me with twenty dudes from Queensbridge. I was excited to see him because we hadn't spoken in a couple months. Then he got closer. His teeth were clenched, and his brow was furrowed. He walked toward me aggressively, like he was about to start some serious shit.

"You think you better than me?" he shouted, as his nostrils flared. "What's up? You think you better, nigga?"

"Man, what the fuck you talkin' about?" I responded, confused as all hell. I was caught completely off guard by his aggressiveness. I thought we were friends. I mean, we had just played together the previous summer. We had gone 59–1 with Riverside and bonded almost every day.

Ron didn't back down and I was ready for it to go down.

"I'm the best player in this city," Artest exclaimed. "Don't forget that shit."

Then . . . he simply walked away with his crew in tow. I was looking around, trying to figure out what just happened. I knew competition for the title of best player in the city was fierce. I knew the status it brought. It came with girls, money, fame, and scholarship offers. But mostly it came with respect. You couldn't put a price on that, and it had to be earned. And Ron was damn willing to earn it. For a lot of these guys, it was all they had. Only one player a year gets the title of best player in New York City, and I sure as hell wasn't going to give it to Ron. No matter how many dudes he had with him. I left the park confused about my encounter, thinking about what it might be like the next time I saw him.

Several weeks later, I was at another AAU tournament with the Panthers in New Jersey. It was one of the last events of the summer, so all the big names were there. If you've ever been to an AAU tournament or summer camp you know that when you walk into the gym, it's wall-to-wall basketball. There can be as many as six games going on side by side with college coaches and scouts moving from court to court.

We were on court four, and my old Riverside teammate Ron Artest was all the way over on court one. I hadn't seen him since our encounter at Riverbank, so I knew to stay on my guard.

Our game was getting increasingly physical with every possession. We were way more talented than our opponent, but they tried to make up for it with their aggression. I was matched up with one of the best prospects in the city, a moody six-foot-ten banger named James Felton who had already committed to Florida State. I was getting the best of him and let him know it with a few choice words.

Early in the game, I grabbed a hard-fought rebound and tossed an outlet pass forty feet downcourt. Everyone raced the other way except for me and Felton.

After I threw the outlet, he reared around and dropped a devastating elbow to my face. I fell to the ground. Since the action had moved downcourt, no one noticed me writhing on the floor. Well, almost no one.

Three courts away, Ron Artest, who was just at my throat a few weeks before, saw what had happened and was not pleased. He dropped everything—despite the fact that his game was in progress—and sprinted toward me across two courts, both with games going on.

I was on the ground, bleeding profusely from my nose. He rushed the court with both of his fists balled up and raised high. He was foaming at the mouth and ready for war. "Who the fuck hit Lamar?" he demanded.

He was there to knock someone the fuck out. I was in a daze from the elbow, the blood spilling, and Ron's cocked fists. It took me a moment or two to figure out what was happening.

That's when everyone else stopped in the middle of the play and rushed back down the court. We were on the brink of a melee. Coaches, referees, and tournament officials scrambled to restore order.

When everything settled down, by some miracle, no one was ejected, but I was out with a broken nose. "No one fucks with Lamar," shouted Artest. "You hear me? No one fucks with my man!"

I told you Ron was a complicated guy, but if nothing else, he's one of the most loyal people I've ever met.

Ron coming to my rescue made me aware for the first time how closely tied together we all were as we tried to navigate the world of high school basketball. We all played a role in each other's story. Even James Felton, the guy who elbowed me in the face. Back in the middle of the summer of 1996, before my senior year, when we were all at ABCD camp at Fairleigh Dickinson, something happened that would change the course of Felton's life. Looking back, this episode kind of explains why he reacted so aggressively to my trash talk.

While the unknown Tracy McGrady was in the middle of his meteoric rise that summer, his team faced off against Felton's in the Outstanding Seniors Game, which closes out the week at ABCD. The court was cluttered with future pros such as Quentin Richardson, Al Harrington, and me. None of us had ever heard of McGrady or his hometown of Auburndale, Florida, before that week. Sonny Vaccaro had done a favor for a coach who was a longtime friend to get Tracy into the camp.

Felton, on the other hand, was a top-twenty-five prospect from nearby Jersey City who was fielding offers from St. John's and Syracuse and who most had pegged as a future pro. With the tiny gym packed to the gills, in a flash, McGrady scooped up a loose ball in the open court and raced for what looked to be an uncontested dunk. But Felton gave chase and jumped with Tracy, who had a forty-two-inch vertical. That was the wrong thing to do.

BOOM!

Tracy thundered down a nasty windmill dunk that ignited the small gym with a raucous celebration, sending spectators pouring out onto the floor and halting the game for five minutes. It was the cherry on top of T-Mac's blistering summer. For Felton, it was one of the most embarrassing moments of his life. From that point, Tracy would go on to win every accolade a high school player could win, declare for the draft, and sign with Adidas.

Meanwhile, Felton fell down a rabbit hole of self-loathing and shame. He started drinking and his behavior became more and more erratic. Eventually, he accepted a scholarship to St. John's, where he, ironically, became close with fellow freshman Ron Artest. After bouncing around professional basketball's minor leagues, he became disillusioned with the sport, took a job as a security guard in Jersey City, and focused on raising his three children.

Felton's health was failing as his years of drinking had damaged his liver, and he developed diabetic neuropathy, which affected the nerves in his size-sixteen feet. One morning, his wife found him dead in bed at the age of twenty-seven.

Sometimes I think about the moment at that tournament in New Jersey and how all of our paths crossed and recrossed time after time. James, Ron, and Lamar. The three biggest high school basketball standouts in the city and what we all had in common, which time will likely forget. People looked at us as basketball stars. Colleges saw us as tickets to the Final Four. Sneaker companies saw us as future pitchmen.

But in truth, all three of us were kids from the New York area who suffered from one form or other of mental illness or substance abuse, or both. But those things were either buried deep beneath the surface or dismissed altogether. I didn't know it yet, but you can't run from the pain forever. Sooner or later it catches you. For Felton, it happened sooner. Too soon.

We were damaged and undiagnosed. To the machinery of basketball, each of us was nothing more than a temporary commodity.

They sold us a dream and we bought it.

9

In the summer of 1996, several weeks after ABCD camp, Sonny Vaccaro and Adidas concocted a master plan for me. They wanted me to transfer to Mount Zion Christian Academy, a prep school in Durham, North Carolina, for my senior year, where I would team up with Tracy McGrady. Mount Zion was a small, fly-by-night boarding school that basically existed to have a basketball team. At the time, there were twenty-five students, tops. The plan would accomplish several things. First, it would take me out of a Nike school, Christ the King, and put me in an Adidas program. Next, it would be the biggest high school basketball story of the year, generating huge press for Sonny and Adidas as we made our way through a national schedule and televised games with tons of media at every stop. Mount Zion would have been the clear-cut favorite to win the coveted national championship that went to the team that finished number one in the final *USA Today* Boys Basketball National Rankings. And more often than not, that team went undefeated.

If I went to Mount Zion, the endgame was simple: Sonny would have the three best young stars in the game draped in Adidas: Kobe, T-Mac, and me. The windfall for Sonny would have been huge. He would have made Adidas officially the biggest player in all of amateur basketball, thereby completing his revenge for his ugly firing from Nike, whose grassroots program he had built and led until 1991.

Sonny wanted to take over the world and this was how he'd do it.

The plan was for Tracy and me to go straight to the NBA once we were done at Mount Zion and sign huge sneaker contracts with Adidas. That meant I would become the youngest person, at seventeen, ever to play in the NBA.

I didn't want to go. No matter how big Sonny's master plan was, I had never been away from home for a long time and had no desire to start now. I also didn't want to leave Christ the King. I liked going there and the idea of attending CTK for all four years of high school appealed to me. There was no better competition in the country than CHSAA. Plus, I was dying to get back to the title game and capture another championship. But really, at the core of everything, I just didn't want to leave my grandmother. It had been only four years since I lost my mother, and I was nowhere near getting over her. I needed my grandmother. I needed home.

There was also the matter of Liza. We were just starting to get to know each other. She wasn't into the basketball scene and never came to the games, but we started hanging out a lot in the summer before my senior year. She had no idea about these plans to go to Mount Zion and was really upset when she heard I might go. She questioned my feelings for her, and I could tell that her trust in me had waned. She was hurt, and I decided to avoid her so I didn't have to face any kind of confrontation. *Just avoid it, Lamar.* That's what I told myself. That began a pattern of dealing with conflict in my life that would last twenty years . . . and to be honest, continues to this day.

At some point, Sonny, always persuasive and persistent, convinced me to go, but I had one condition: I didn't want to go alone. I asked Greg Nunn to go with me. Even though he had graduated in the spring, Sonny and Gary could hook up his prep year easily enough. Greg agreed to go, especially since a year at a prep school would better prepare him to play in college. And just like that we were headed to Mount Zion. Tracy was already enrolled and getting settled in. I had never seen Sonny so excited as he watched his master plan unfold just as he'd envisioned.

I backed out on the Tuesday before Greg and I were to leave for North Carolina. Greg was pissed.

"What do you mean you're not going?" he shouted at me on the sidewalk in front of my house. "Well, if you're not going, then I'm not going either."

"Man, it's my bad, but I can't leave," I reasoned.

"You fucked me."

He had a right to be pissed. All I had to do was head straight back to the familiar surroundings of Christ the King and stay on the path I was already on. He didn't enroll in college or another prep school because he had committed to Mount Zion. He had no other options.

Gary was furious, too, because he felt he'd let Sonny down and couldn't collect on delivering me to him. But he couldn't be that mad because it really wasn't a bad situation for him. I still played for his Adidas-sponsored Panthers, he was getting money from many other sources, and he knew he would have a hand in my college decision. Sonny also got over it pretty quickly, and I enrolled back at Christ the King.

Over the next few weeks, I began to feel more depressed than usual. Even though I was happy to be staying home, I just kept thinking about my mother. Wondering why she was taken from me. Not having any answers while keeping everything bottled inside. I had always felt a deep, raw, almost crippling sadness since she passed, but now I was having trouble keeping all my emotions in check. I survived by pushing it down, and when I started to feel like it was no longer working, the only thing I wanted to do was hide. Disappear from the rest of the world.

I would stay in my room a lot or hide away with close friends. Liza always knew what to say, and even though she got over her frustration with me, I couldn't shake the feeling of depression.

I started skipping school. A lot of it. In the first sixteen days of my senior year, I only attended twice. I didn't complete a single assignment or so much as crack open a book. It was only September, and I was already in jeopardy of being academically disqualified for my senior season.

Gary was again furious with me.

"They're gonna fail you off the fucking team!" he exclaimed.

I wasn't worried about it. Gary would think of something. He had too much riding on my success.

Gary ended up finding a prep school for Greg called Redemption Christian Academy in Troy, New York. It was about 160 miles upstate in the middle of nowhere and not that different from Mount Zion. It was a bare-bones boarding school where it seemed like the administrators made up the rules as they went along. The place was a dump.

It wasn't all bad for Greg, however. Early in the summer, Gary paid for Greg to take a summer-school class at a college preparatory school in New York. Gary had a hookup where someone could just sign Greg in so he didn't need to attend the class or do any work. That way he could still attend tournaments in Las Vegas and California. Now, all Greg had to do was finish the one prep season at Redemption and he'd be qualified academically to attend college without having to stay for the whole school year.

Eventually, I had dug myself too big a hole with my absences and failing grades. Greg convinced my grandmother to pull me out of Christ the King, and then he shipped me off to, you guessed it, Redemption Christian Academy.

First, I called Greg at Redemption.

"How is it up there?" I asked.

"It's a real shithole," he said. "You'll fit in great."

We both laughed. I hung up and three days later, without even letting Liza know where I was going, I was in upstate New York, surrounded by nothingness and chaos. I thought Greg had been kidding.

The place was an unorganized circus. It was a fledgling boarding school that was falling apart. How the hell did Gary find this place? There was no heat in our room or the classrooms. When students arrived, they had to make their own bunk beds out of two-by-fours. The food tasted like cardboard. We did everything ourselves but grow our own crops. There were forty kids sharing three showers. If the hot water ran out, you were shit out of luck.

Of course, Gary and Greg failed to tell me any of this. Greg was still pissed over the Mount Zion fiasco, and I guess this was his way of payback. I knew as soon as I saw the place that I was gone the moment the buzzer sounded after the season's last game.

The founder of Redemption was Pastor John Massey Jr. He was a real wildcard, praise-the-Lord type whose shiftiness seem to fit in perfectly with the rest of the amateur basketball world. He had a cordial griminess and took advantage of having one of the top ballers in the country at his school.

He founded the school in 1979, but it hardly had a reputation for basketball and couldn't be found on the basketball map with a magnifying glass. The year prior to our arrival, future Georgetown star Victor Page occupied the same halls that we would.

Once I got up there, Greg and I were assigned to the same room. We immediately established rule and took the place over. It felt like a lockup, so we ran the school like a jail. Greg was the hardnosed prison guard and I was the laid-back, soft-hearted warden. The students were in awe because they had never met someone they'd seen in newspapers before. There was a group of African students who called me "MVP" and would hit me up for autographs and advice.

Greg started to get a little too into it.

"I'm running this school," he declared. "Nobody can fight unless I say so. Nobody can get extra food unless I say so."

It wasn't mean-spirited, but that's what that place sort of did to us. We were New York City boys and we talked big. It just sort of happened. We didn't want to be there. Everything felt like a survival exercise.

Meanwhile, Pastor Massey was up to his own backroom dealings. He'd let low-level agents fly me in private jets to AAU tournaments in Florida and keep it hush-hush. It's like we were just checking off NCAA violations on purpose.

Greg was assigned by Gary to be his man on the inside: to keep watch over me and report back with everything that related to Lamar Odom, particularly if Massey was involved. The information Greg provided kept Gary and Sonny abreast of the situation, despite the fact they were hundreds of miles away.

While Gary and Sonny were looking out for their interest in me—making sure no one got too close or influenced my thinking—Pastor Massey began to do the same. In other words, he wanted to prevent Greg from being Gary's informant in order to protect *his* newfound interest in me. There was a lot of money to go around, but college coaches were highly motivated to limit their payments to just Gary.

With me in his stable, Pastor Massey became a very important person in the basketball community, if only for a while. NBA teams started to call with cash offers to set up private workouts. This was a huge no-no, and both Gary and Greg were vehemently opposed to setting up these clandestine workouts. There was nothing to gain. The problem was that Gary couldn't tell Massey he knew without compromising Greg's status as a spy.

With everything swirling around me, it was actually becoming more and more like prison culture with everyone looking over his shoulder while trafficking in a very valuable commodity: information.

Our only way to communicate with Gary was with a pay phone in the school lobby, which we were certain Pastor Massey had tapped. After one call home, Greg was suspended for a week without explanation. It was Massey's way of getting to me without Greg's watchful eyes. It also effectively cut Gary out of the equation while Greg was on a bus for the four-hour trip back to Queens.

Of course, Gary was getting frustrated, and after Greg's second suspension, he threatened to pull me out of school. When Greg returned, Massey separated us as dorm mates and bunked him up with a supervisor.

"Man, I feel like I'm in the hole," I remember him saying.

At the time, I was heavy into my recruitment with UNLV, and our main contact was an assistant coach and recruiting coordinator named Greg "Shoes" Vetrone, a tough basketball lifer from my home borough.

Shoes had a cozy relationship with Gary and had been on the recruiting scene for nearly twenty years. His ties with Gary had been scrutinized by many media outlets and basketball insiders over the years. Regardless of what Shoes was doing, he was not a big fan of Massey and felt (rightly so) that the pastor was using me to hustle him and line his own pockets.

One day in early 1997, Shoes flew to New York and picked Greg and me up from Redemption. He warned us about Massey, but we were already leery of him. Well, at least everyone around me was. I never let this sort of stuff bother me too much. I had become so used to being hustled, bought, and sold by adults that nothing was very much of a surprise. And I was never opposed to having a wad of cash in my pocket.

In the car on the way to a restaurant where Shoes was taking us, he picked up his car phone and dialed Pastor Massey. "I'm gonna show you what he's really up to," said Shoes with a voice like something out of *The Sopranos*.

He put the phone on speaker. Massey picked up his home phone with no idea we were in the car. Vetrone was concerned about my grades. I was struggling badly, and Shoes wanted to make sure I was going to be eligible next fall by the time I got to college.

"The good Lord is going to make sure Lamar has his grades," said Massey, as if reassuring a large congregation.

But it seems the Lord worked on retainer. After that call, which just proved to Greg and me that Massey was crooked, it seemed I needed three grades changed. And Massey wanted $15,000 for three Bs. And so it was done. At the end of the week I had my report card filled with fraudulent As and Bs. By that time, the living conditions had become unbearable. Greg and I got what we needed: report cards indicating that we were college eligible. Despite the fact there were two weeks left in the season, we left Redemption. But to our surprise, when Redemption sent my transcripts, I saw nothing but Fs. I had been had. And so had Greg. We weren't eligible to play in college.

Gary quickly arranged for me to enroll at St. Thomas Aquinas, a prep school in New Britain, Connecticut, whose boys' team was coached by his longtime friend Jerry DeGregorio.

Despite how tumultuous, confusing, and uncomfortable my last year in high school was, I still ended up with a truck-load of honors. In the spring of 1997, I was named *Parade* All-America First Team for the second year in a row, including being named National Player of the Year. I also received invites to the McDonald's All-American Game as well as the Adidas-backed Magic's Roundball Classic.

My high school career was finally over. I won't lie, a little bit of sadness came over me, but I was excited about what lay ahead. I was ready. And even if I wasn't, there was no turning back.

Although I never even played at the last school of my three-high-school senior year, something sticks out. St. Thomas Aquinas, established in 1955, with its red-brick façade, now sits abandoned on an overgrown lot. An empty building, it is now home to discarded school desks, ancient science equipment, and rusty lockers. On the wall of the art room was a mural with a mountainous landscape against a blue sky over which read "Climb high, expand your horizons."

That's exactly what I planned to do.

10

Less than a year before, it had been Sonny's grand plan to unite me and Tracy McGrady. So, it felt kind of ironic that in my final high school game, I would be matched up against T-Mac.

In the spring of 1997, at the end of my senior year, I headed to Auburn Hills, Michigan, to play in Magic's Roundball Classic, an All-American showcase that Sonny sponsored. There would be at least a half-dozen future NBA players putting on a show. Naturally, Sonny put Tracy and me on opposite teams and breathlessly hyped the showdown in the weeks leading up to the game.

But the would-be storied matchup fizzled. McGrady played like the best player in the country. Damn, he looked like an NBA All-Star. He knocked down pull-ups, hit threes, made ridiculous passes in transition, and was on the receiving end of one highlight alley-oop dunk after another. One particular play stands out in my mind to this day. I controlled a left-handed dribble at the top of the key, hit T-Mac with a head fake, and blew by him. I had nothing but space in front of me. Opportunity was calling on me to throw it down with authority.

I just couldn't elevate for some reason, so I laid the ball up softly with my left hand. Out of nowhere McGrady swooped in and swatted the shot, which ricocheted violently off the backboard. In a microcosm of the game, McGrady got the rebound and was off and running to orchestrate another high-light fast break while I stood and argued with the ref. What's more, McGrady seemed to develop an instant rapport with the speedy six-foot point guard Greedy Daniels, as if they had played together all their lives. Greedy had just committed to UNLV and wondered if I was going to join him.

"What's the deal? You coming to Vegas?" asked Greedy earlier that week.

"That's what I'm trying to figure out," I said. "I'm going to decide soon, I think."

"You know we need you, man. Let's do it."

Truth is, I didn't want to think about it. Big decisions intim-idated me, and I tried to avoid them as best I could. There was a lot of pressure, people constantly in my ear, and the fear of making the wrong decision gnawed at me. Regret seemed to linger with me, and I didn't want to add to the existing pile of woes.

Meanwhile, big decisions weren't a problem for McGrady. Although he was quiet and reserved off the floor, he had a certain swag and confidence about him. Shortly after he daz-zled his way to MVP honors at Magic's Roundball Classic, McGrady confidently declared for the draft. From complete unknown to future NBA star in nine months. I was in awe, but I had my own future to figure out.

In fact, that very weekend in Michigan I was going to make my college decision. My family flew out. Gary Charles and Greg Nunn made the trip. I had no idea where I wanted to play my college ball.

Sonny, Gary, Greg, and a group of family members gathered in my hotel room. On the counter in the bathroom of the suite were four hats: Kentucky, UNLV, UConn, and a Knicks hat representing the NBA. I had to go in the bathroom, lock the door, make a decision, and then come out wearing one of the hats.

Everyone in the room offered their opinions about where I should go. Gary liked Kentucky. So did one of my family members, largely because they had accepted money from the school. Greg and Sonny wanted me to go straight to the NBA, which, back then, didn't happen very often. I wanted the college experience, as I was looking forward to a year or two of bulking up and playing against tougher competition.

I went into the bathroom and shut the door behind me. I didn't want to look at the hats. I stood in front of the mirror and looked at myself. *Who am I?* I thought. I often struggled with that question. I only knew that I didn't have much of an answer. Would I find answers in one of the hats? Would one of them make me a complete person? Would I satisfy people? Would I disappoint them? What if I lifted up one of the hats only to find more regret? Would the things I'd done come back to haunt me? Or worse, the people I loved?

I let out a breath and turned on the faucet to splash water on my face. I looked at myself with the water dripping off my cheeks. It made me look like I was crying. Was I actually crying? I wanted to feel something and nothing at the exact same time. Again, that would become a recurring theme in my life.

I didn't want to put any of the hats on, because I didn't want to make a decision. I flipped the seat down, sat on the toilet, and stared straight ahead. I paced back and forth. I lay in the tub. I curled up on the floor. I did push-ups. Splashed more water on my face. I tried to picture myself winning a national championship. It would have made a great movie montage.

But mostly I pictured my mom, Cathy. She would know what to do.

"Just be nice to everyone," she would tell me. "Go with what's in your heart."

Outside in the hotel room, I could hear people coming and going. No one ever knocked on the door. I must have been in there for two hours.

I picked up the Kentucky hat and stared at it.

In December of my junior year at Christ the King, Kentucky played Iona at Madison Square Garden. Kentucky coach Rick Pitino scheduled the game so I could see them up close. They were the number-two team in the country and had a roster full of killers. Antoine Walker. Derek Anderson. Tony Delk. Ron Mercer. Four NBA players right there. They drilled Iona 106–79 as we sat in the front row. Kentucky won the national championship that year, making Rick Pitino's pitch even easier.

The reality is, I knew exactly where I wanted to go: UCLA. But there was no Bruins hat on the counter . . . for a reason.

Okay, let's back up.

Five months before, to the day. That's when the course of my life and basketball career quietly changed. UCLA head coach Jim Harrick was fired for covering up details about an improper dinner. He had taken star twin centers Jason and

Jarron Collins from Los Angeles, and Earl Watson from Kansas City, out to a recruiting dinner along with several members of the coaching staff and five current UCLA players including Jelani McCoy, Cameron Dollar, and present Golden State Warriors general manager Bob Myers.

Harrick's trouble began shortly after he filed an outsized expense report for the dinner for thousands of dollars that caught the eye of the athletic department. At the time, UCLA's athletic director, Peter Dalis, called it the biggest expense report he'd seen in fourteen years.

The whole thing centered around the fact that there were two more players at the dinner than the NCAA allowed. Dalis accused Harrick of falsifying the expense report to cover his tracks. Harrick fought the allegations and swore Dalis had it out for him. In the end, Harrick was dismissed. He wasn't happy. He let his feelings be known at his farewell press conference.

"The punishment doesn't fit the crime," said Harrick. "Dalis has been after me for years. I'm not saying I'm not at fault. If it was unethical, I apologize. Sometimes I use poor judgment. But it's no violation. I just feel the punishment is too much."

Either way Harrick was out. And so was I. That's why there was no UCLA hat in the bathroom that day.

Fourteen days after Harrick's dismissal, I signed two NCAA letters of intent: one with UNLV and one with UConn. Signing two was highly unusual, but it bought me time and prevented me from having to make a decision then. Funny enough, the next day I played my first game for Redemption Christian in front of coaches from UNLV and UConn and rang up twenty-four points and fifteen rebounds.

But back in that bathroom, I had to make a decision. I came out holding the UNLV hat. I still didn't want to put it on.

Then it was time to do the press conference, which would be my formal announcement to the world. Gary took the hat and put it in a custom-made Adidas bag. Then he started to prepare for the announcement. He called UNLV head coach Bill Bayno and his assistant Shoes Vetrone with the good news. But more importantly, he had to call Rick Pitino, who was fully expecting me to come to Kentucky and would not be happy with the latest development. But Pitino was nowhere to be found, and Gary was stressing like mad.

The press conference was to take place in the Pistons' locker room with sports commentator great Dick Vitale conducting the interview. Gary walked up and saw Sonny and Dickie V talking. Now, Gary was decked out in a four-button suit with one of his trademark fedoras. Gary loved to roll in style. He must have had a dozen of those suits and twice as many hats. Vitale was adamant, however, that Gary take off the hat when on TV.

"You can't wear that hat on TV," exclaimed Vitale. "You'll look like some kind of mobster or drug dealer."

Gary, who was a vice president at Citibank on Wall Street, was furious and refused to take off the hat. All of a sudden, a three-way argument broke out about a hat. And it wasn't even my UNLV hat! I guess it was a strange and fitting end to my recruitment.

After I made the announcement and did the interview with Vitale, it felt like a weight had been lifted off my shoulders. Everyone made plans for dinner to celebrate. Gary excused himself to use the bathroom. As he was standing at the urinal,

Aunt JaNean stormed in and grabbed Gary by the throat. Gary's pants were hanging down and JaNean was livid. What a mess.

"You're in the men's room! What the hell is wrong with you?" shouted Gary.

"This better be some kind of joke," screamed JaNean.

She was angry that I didn't go to Kentucky and that Gary's fingerprints were all over the UNLV deal. But they made up two weeks later when it was announced that Pitino left Kentucky for the Boston Celtics.

And with that, my high school career officially ended, and the spotlight would only get brighter, the stakes bigger, and the pressure more intense.

I needed to go home.

Liza and I had stayed in touch, and when I got back to New York, we met up for a slice of pizza. Since my senior year was so chaotic and disjointed, I almost completely forgot the normal rhythm of the everyday high school experience.

"I can't believe it's almost over and prom is coming up," Liza said, catching me off guard. I had completely forgotten about prom.

"Who are you going with?" I asked sheepishly.

"No one really."

"Do you want me to go with you?"

"Yeah, sure. Okay."

I was happy she agreed because I felt like I could make it up to her for leaving Christ the King without even telling her.

She was totally in the dark when I left and found out through friends. She had no idea about the drama I was going through and didn't forgive me for months. I was embarrassed that I was flunking out, so I just couldn't face telling her. I really wanted that moment at prom with her. I had such great memories at Christ the King and made so many good friends that I deeply hoped to end on a happy note. I needed to feel normal, and going to prom was just about the most normal thing I'd ever do in high school.

The prom for the graduating class of 1997 was held at a fancy hall in Flushing Meadows, Queens. When I saw Liza in her dress, I thought she looked like an angel. Royal blue was her favorite color, and she had spent the day getting her hair done. I was so excited to see friends I hadn't seen for so long that it felt like we spent the entire night catching up. People peppered me with questions about UNLV, but I didn't want the night to be about me. I wanted one night where I didn't have to be *that* Lamar Odom. There was a professional photographer in the back, and we took several pictures to freeze the moment in time. At the end of the night, everyone got out on the dance floor to cut loose one more time.

I officially ended my high school experience slow dancing with my arms wrapped around the girl I intended to marry.

11

left for UNLV in June 1997, not long after graduating from high school. I was cleared to play academically and couldn't wait to meet my new teammates and get on the court. UNLV's roster my freshman year was a bomb squad that featured three future NBA players and a couple guys who ended up playing overseas. Smooth-shooting small forward Tyrone Nesby would be a teammate of mine with the Clippers. Keon Clark was a lanky seven-foot shot-blocking terror. Louisiana-bred point guard Greedy Daniels was one of the fastest players in the country. And my former Christ the King teammate Kevin Simmons rounded out what prognosticators considered a surefire Sweet 16 team that would bring UNLV back to relevance.

One thing I forgot to mention.

During my senior year, it was arranged that someone would take my SATs for me to ensure my college eligibility. I rarely studied or devoted time to schoolwork, but of more concern, I just wasn't a good test taker. My inability to concentrate always seemed to get in the way when I sat down to take a test. The SATs were an enormous obstacle, which I dreaded.

The test confused me. There were so many things in the test booklet I simply didn't know because I had never been taught them. But even still, I couldn't concentrate when sitting down at a desk with a No. 2 pencil, trying to fill out A, B, C, or D.

I had never been diagnosed with attention-deficit/hyper-activity disorder (ADHD). The world I came from didn't even know it existed. But if you described it to me at sixteen I would've known exactly what it was.

But then again, I've lived my entire life undiagnosed. I was judged by my performance on a playing field that I shouldn't have been on. Anytime I was presented with work that confused me or I wasn't prepared for, an alternative was set up by someone who had a stake in my future. I said yes to those alternatives every time.

The guy who took the SATs for me didn't get caught, but he did make a crucial mistake that would ultimately end my college career at UNLV before it started.

"He scored too fucking high!" raged Gary. "A 1200? Are you fucking kidding me? Lamar's a C student! What, is he going to the Ivy League?"

Back in the spring of 1997, just before the Roundball Classic, I was asked to do a favor for an old friend of Sonny Vaccaro's, former UNLV head coach Jerry Tarkanian. He was trying to resurrect his career at Fresno State after a bitter divorce from UNLV five years earlier. Tarkanian wanted me to make an official visit to Fresno State. No one had any delusions that I would sign with Fresno; it was just to show people, especially high school players, that Tark could still recruit with the best. Getting the number-one player in the country to commit to an official visit would do the trick.

I never made the visit, and of course, Tarkanian was not pleased that I spurned him. Several weeks before the start of classes at UNLV, a *Sports Illustrated* article reported that the NCAA was calling into question the validity of my SAT scores. This was not good. It was highly unusual for an SAT score to be looked into once a player signed a letter of intent and enrolled in school.

In my mind (then and now), there was only one conclusion: there had to be a snitch. To a man, although we couldn't prove it, everyone in my circle believed Tarkanian dropped a dime and ratted me out to the NCAA as payback for not giving him a courtesy visit. It was his way to hit back at UNLV . . . and me.

UNLV rescinded my scholarship. This was one of the darkest days of my life. All these years of shrugging things off and taking the easy way out, avoiding confrontation and not wanting to do the work, finally came back to bite me.

UNLV head coach Bill Bayno cried when he told his assistant Shoes Vetrone the news. Shoes broke down, too. But neither of them had the courage to deliver the information to me themselves. They sent another assistant, who I had almost no contact with, to drop off an official letter.

Barry "Slice" Worsen was a thirty-seven-year-old assistant from Brooklyn who once had a walk-on role in the movie *Glengarry Glen Ross* with Al Pacino. He had this thing where he called everybody "judge." He knocked on the door and I answered. He spoke in a low, quiet voice. It was awkward because I had never dealt with him directly before.

"Hey, judge, I'm sorry to have to do this," he said as he handed me the envelope, "but this is for you."

I couldn't talk my way out of this one. Nobody could. What made these days even more difficult was that Gary and Sonny, the people who were in this with me, who knowingly risked my career, wouldn't even speak to me. I sat in my apartment in the dark alone for days and cried. It was 116 degrees outside, but I was in the coldest place on earth. I tried for two days to get ahold of Gary and Sonny with no luck. Where were they?

They had to know what was going on—this was too big not to know. But why weren't they reaching out to me? I felt like I didn't have a friend in the world and was without a clue as to what my next move would be. I felt betrayed. I felt small, mad, angry, upset. But mostly, I felt alone. Without a future on a college team, my life was broken. I couldn't go anywhere. I didn't have a car. I didn't have any money. My feelings of abandonment, which I was constantly fighting off, overtook me. I was supposed to be this big-time basketball star, and guys like that don't go to people with issues about their feelings. I wasn't allowed to be vulnerable. So, I once again turned inward and self-medicated with weed.

One of the few people who was there for me in those dark days was David Chapman, a prominent Las Vegas dentist and businessman, as well as a UNLV booster who had a burning passion for all things Rebels. Soon after my dismissal, I moved out of my apartment and into David's house. He gave me a place to stay, put money in my pocket, and reassured me that everything would be all right.

One night, while wallowing in my own pity, I decided I needed a pick-me-up. David let me borrow his car, and I just drove to get my mind off everything. The fact that I didn't have a license didn't really matter to me. I picked up a couple forty-ounce beers and went cruising. I was looking for company. A young, handsome guy in a high-end BMW? Forty-ounce beer in his lap? Nothing left to lose? What could go wrong?

Feeling impatient and not in the mood to sweet-talk my way into someone's heart, I was ready to pay for my company. After a short while I picked up an attractive young woman and we began to hit it off.

It was too good to be true. She was an undercover Las Vegas cop. She arrested me as soon as I started negotiating her fee.

It was a heck of a few days for the nation's top recruit: kicked out of UNLV, abandoned by friends, arrested for solicitation. With my head held low, I called David to bail me out. My voice was shaky and weak, and it cracked as I explained what had happened. It was the first time I was ever arrested. I felt like a failure.

I knew the shady dealings with UNLV were going to follow me around until I went pro. But since I had already missed the cutoff to declare for the NBA draft, I didn't have much of a choice but to stay in school. Not only did scandal follow me around, it also caught up with Greg. When he arrived at St. Francis in Queens to play ball his freshman year, the NCAA's investigative team paid him a surprise visit and questioned him for six hours.

They wanted to know about the gear that UNLV had been sending us while we were at Redemption. They had pictures of

Greg wearing the clothes. The thing about cash is that when it disappears, it's untraceable. The same cannot be said about a hooded sweatshirt.

Greg's coaches prepped him for his NCAA interview with one simple piece of advice: if you're about to tell a lie, just say, "I do not recall." He did not recall forty-nine times.

12

needed to get out of Vegas as fast as humanly possible. My UNLV experience had been a complete disaster. I needed a new start.

I didn't know where I was going to go, and after a thawing-out period, I was back to working with Gary Charles and Sonny Vaccaro on my next move. Gary had eventually reached out to me after the UNLV disaster, and in my mind, even though I forgave Gary and Sonny, I never truly forgot.

Because time was short, my options were limited. It was late August 1997, and most schools had already committed their allotment of scholarships. Besides, few would touch me given what had happened.

So, an old face came back into the picture. Sonny got on the phone with Jim Harrick, the former UCLA coach, who was now the head coach at the University of Rhode Island in the Atlantic 10 Conference. After a few more phone calls and filling out the necessary paperwork, I was off to Kingston, Rhode Island. But there was a catch. There's always a catch. Gary wanted Rhode Island to hire Jerry DeGregorio as an assistant coach. After the Vegas fiasco, both Gary and Sonny wanted someone to look after me on a daily basis to make sure I stayed below the radar. That someone was Jerry.

He and I got along well, and I really felt like he had my best interests at heart. He was like the white father I never had. Jerry got set up at Rhode Island, and Sonny had his fingerprints all over everything. They hired a lawyer to help with the admissions process.

Once all of Gary's wrangling and dealings with the lawyer were done, there was still one more step. In a meeting with the university president, Dr. Robert Carothers, some basketball staff, and a handful of alumni, I was quizzed on various topics, from my background to what I could bring to the table if I was admitted. The meeting felt strange to me, as if all these people were prodding me with questions because they didn't believe in me. After answering everything, I could see they were not convinced. They had one of the best players in the country in their meeting room, but it wasn't enough.

Then, they asked me to write an essay about my life right there in the room and then read it back to them. It was clear to me that they didn't think I could read or write. I was humiliated. This grade-school exercise disgusted and embarrassed me. After all I'd been through, all of the low points, each day seemed to bring me a step closer to rock bottom. After reading a page and a half of my handwritten essay, I just stopped. There was an awkward silence in the room as people looked around at one another, shocked that I could read.

As humiliating an experience as that was, I made it through and was admitted to Rhode Island as a non-matriculating (unofficial) student. I had to sit out the first semester of my freshman season and maintain a 2.4 grade-point average to be eligible to play in the spring. Even though I agreed to the conditions, being without basketball for the first time in my life sent me on an emotional tailspin.

I was so depressed that for the first time, I had to get professional help. I went to a doctor who put me through a series of tests. He then put me on Prozac, an antidepressant, to treat my depression and anxiety. I knew I was down, but I thought I was just sad. Even when things were looking up, I'd still feel like I was in a haze, and I couldn't figure out why. I just thought it was my mood. I really didn't know or understand what depression was. I could feel the positive effects of the Prozac as the weeks went by. It calmed me down and kept me sane. I stayed on the drug the entire semester.

Once I finally got settled in at school, the pickup games in Keaney Gymnasium, our 3,800-seat home court, provided a much-needed distraction. I really wanted to experience campus life, and I became a social butterfly. Every day we'd eat at the Ram's Den, the food court, in Memorial Union on campus. On Tuesdays and Thursdays, we'd hit the local college bars.

I didn't particularly like going to class, but my African American Studies class kept me engaged. I felt like a regular college kid. Soon I began to realize how much better the quiet, leafy green splendor of Kingston was for me than the bright lights and pulsating heart of Las Vegas would have been. Rhode Island's small-town, close-knit vibe was exactly what I needed, even as I continued to isolate whenever I felt alone or overwhelmed.

I've had separation anxiety since my mother died, although back then I didn't know there was a name for it. I hated to be alone. The feeling that no one was around and that I'd been abandoned could easily trigger the pain of my mother's death, which constantly lingered, haunting both my dreams and my waking hours. To this day, I find it ironic that when things get the darkest, I choose to be alone. I retreat to where no one can find me. At URI, this happened often enough. I'd hide in my room or at a friend's on the other side of campus. Anywhere to be away from the mess my life had become.

It was when I was back on the court with the ball in my hands that I felt somewhat like my old self. And I absolutely loved being around the guys on the team.

Cuttino "Cat" Mobley was a below-the-radar, lefty senior shooting guard who was a fountain of constant energy and positivity. He had fashioned himself into an NBA prospect and was the captain of the team. No one at Rhode Island did more to keep my spirits buoyed than Cat. For that, I can never repay him.

Tavorris Bell was a freshman and former teammate of mine from the Long Island Panthers. At a slender six feet six with a forty-four-inch vertical leap, T-Bell was one of the most exciting guys I'd ever played with. He was always a threat to do something on the floor I'd never seen before. I'd known him since I was sixteen, and his hilariously perverse sense of humor was always a welcome respite from the drudgery of depression that hung over me. Whether it was some goofy accent or a character he'd play to get a laugh, there was nobody better to have around to pick me up.

We had some great open runs before the season started. Sometimes we'd head thirty miles north to battle the guys from Providence. Other times they would come to URI. I had some pretty epic battles with Jamel Thomas from Coney Island, who had a brief stint in the NBA. Those pickup games were as cathartic as they were intense. I needed them, and I needed the guys.

But whatever life those runs gave me, it was quickly sucked back out in October during Midnight Madness with the realization that I wasn't going to play until the spring semester.

The guys were jelling as a unit on and off the floor, and even though they kept me involved as much as possible, I still felt left out. I'd regularly find myself in my room in our team apartment at the Graduate Houses, while the rest of the guys were getting ready for the season.

One night in October, I was feeling particularly vulnerable. T-Bell and I were in our suite around eight o'clock in the evening when everything came rushing back: UNLV, my fractured relationship with Sonny, being redshirted, and, as always, my mom. I couldn't shake the feeling of failure. I wanted to get the hell out of Rhode Island. T-Bell was caught off guard by my revelations.

I jumped up and fumbled my way to the kitchen, where I found an unopened bottle of Bacardi Limón. I ripped off the cap, went back into the living room, and sat down on the floor in front of the couch. I took swig after swig. I was eighteen and had never really drunk hard alcohol before. I took the occasional sip of Henny, but that was about it. I had never been drunk. Because I had such a low tolerance, I got drunk really fast that night. My throat burned.

"Why the fuck did this shit happen to me?" I cried out. "All I want to do is play basketball and be happy."

I had downed the entire bottle in less than an hour. I felt warm, delirious, and reckless. But at least I couldn't feel the pain for a while.

"Man, why you still holding on to that bottle," laughed T-Bell.

"I gotta finish it," I drunkenly stammered. "It's up to me."

I clutched the bottle like a pacifier for thirty minutes after I drained its contents. I had to get out of the apartment.

"Take me to The Ghetto," I demanded.

The Ghetto was an area of campus housing where they seemed to put all the students of color. It was actually a nice place, but the veiled segregation wasn't lost on us. There was a sizeable Cape Verdean population, and many of the women were quite beautiful. T-Bell dropped me off at the apartment of a girl named Rose. But I had no idea where I was.

The next thing I knew, the sun was coming up and I was stumbling around behind Rose's building. When T-Bell pulled up, he found me next to the dumpster wearing only a wife beater, boxers, and one sock. I was on my knees puking my guts out. He took me back to our apartment, and I crawled into bed. My head throbbed like a Richter-scale–shattering earthquake. There were aftershocks every ten minutes for hours. The room wouldn't stop spinning, but at least I was in my bed. I stayed there for two days.

The next hiccup came in January 1998, when I was ruled academically ineligible for the spring semester after I failed to maintain a 2.4 GPA. President Carothers released a cold statement:

Lamar Odom is not a student at the University of Rhode Island. He is not an applicant for admission at the University of Rhode Island. I know from talking to him he has the intelligence and the capacity to be successful in college work, and I am very hopeful he will persist in doing the work that is required of him to gain admission to the University of Rhode Island.

Damn. That didn't help. I needed more Prozac.

With me on the sidelines, the team had a great run through the 1998 NCAA Division I Men's Basketball Tournament. The Rams shocked the nation, knocking off Paul Pierce and the number-one-seeded Kansas Jayhawks in the round of thirty-two, behind Cuttino Mobley's twenty-seven points. Rhody made it to its first ever Elite Eight, where we lost to a loaded number-three-seeded Stanford team, which featured three future NBA players.

I was excited for the team's success, but if I'd been eligible, we would have certainly been a Final Four team or possibly national champions. It would have been one of the best college basketball stories of the decade. I felt like I let the team down, but the guys would make sure never to spin it like that.

Once the season ended, I found out that I was again eligible to play because I had gotten the grades. But there was still something gnawing at me. There was still a demon that needed to be exorcised. So, in June I made a weekend trip back to Las Vegas, where I felt I had some unfinished business. When I arrived on campus, the heat rose up from the pavement and distorted the view. But I could see as clearly as ever. I made my way to the gym where UNLV teammates were playing pickup.

The guys were going hard, but one in particular caught my eye. He was a skinny pogo stick with a weird jump shot named Shawn Marion. I'd never heard of him, but he was expected to be a star after transferring from Vincennes University, a junior college in Indiana. He had recently signed his letter of intent with UNLV.

I laced my sneakers, took the court, and walked directly up to Marion. I was locked in. Zoned out. Whoever was in front of me that day, I gave them the business. I was talking more shit than I ever had in my life. Head coach Bill Bayno and assistant coach Shoes Vetrone came down to watch the games. I wanted them to see what they missed out on. I had to let them know.

I'd brought the ball up the court and told my opponents what I was going to do. I called out threes. Broke down my defenders with my crossover. Dunked with absolute power. Threw pinpoint full-court passes. Shawn looked confused at everything I threw at him. The coaches watched in awe. Afterward, I picked up my gym bag and threw a towel around my head. I crossed paths with the coaching staff, exchanged a few cordial words, wished them luck, and headed out into the afternoon sun.

A weight was lifted off my shoulders yet again. My step felt lighter. UNLV and everything that came with it no longer mattered. For the first time in years, I felt free.

13

When I left for UNLV in 1997, Liza was off to John Jay College of Criminal Justice to pursue her love of forensics and criminology. The first time she saw *The Silence of the Lambs*, she knew what her calling was going to be, but she ended up having to put her education on hold.

Late that fall Liza started to feel sick and couldn't pinpoint why she was exhausted and nauseated all the time. Whatever it was, it couldn't wait any longer, and she went to see the doctor, who confirmed her worst fears: She was pregnant. And terrified.

Her mind began to race. How would she tell me? Would she have to drop out of school? How could she afford to have a baby? Was her life over? She believed it was, but most of all, she feared telling her mother, who put nothing over her beloved Catholic faith. Her mom didn't believe in sex before marriage, let alone an unplanned child out of wedlock.

For the first few months of her pregnancy, Liza was a wreck. She went out of her way to hide any sign that she was carrying a child. She cried herself to sleep nearly every night, stopped seeing most of her friends, and lost interest in the things she once loved. Worst of all, she knew that day was coming when she couldn't hide her condition any longer, and she would have to tell her mother. She practiced by telling a childhood friend first but still held out as long as she could. When the day finally came, it did not go as planned. It went way worse. She sat her mom down at the kitchen table and quickly broke the news through tears.

Her mother burst out crying and launched into a screaming fit. She paced back and forth in their small kitchen and prayed.

"What have I done, Lord?" she cried. "Why my child?"

The revelation had a seismic impact on their relationship and their household. Once brimming with love and warmth, it turned cold right along with the seasons. Her mother didn't speak to her for four weeks. They would pass each other in the hallway without so much as a glance. They ate breakfast without exchanging a single word. The news was not treated as a joyous occasion, and Liza worried about her future. I only called when I knew Liza's mom wouldn't be there. If her mother picked up, I hung up.

"I know it's that boy," her mother would say.

When Liza told me, I took the news differently. I was numb, confused at first, but after our initial conversation, my mind was made up.

"I don't want to have an abortion," Liza told me with a soft, determined voice I had never heard before. "I'm serious. I want my baby girl. If you don't feel the same way, I will leave you. Do you?"

I could hear the truth in her quivering voice. It was a mother's love. That was precious to me. I looked at her and imagined what my baby girl would look like. I touched Liza's cheek gently with the back of my hand, and then I pulled her close.

"I want this baby," I told her as my voice cracked. "We're gonna have a baby girl!"

She began to cry. She pressed her face to my chest, leaving tear stains on my shirt. This was my Destiny.

As the summer of 1998 rolled around, and I was figuring out my situation at URI, the stalemate between Liza and her mother began to thaw. Liza was seven months pregnant and making regular visits to the doctor. Liza's mother prayed on it. Soon after, she would devote all her free time to helping Liza raise her granddaughter with love and care—much as she had done with Liza.

I was going to be a father at eighteen years old, and I was about to have some real-life responsibilities that most teens didn't have to worry about. The realities for Liza were much different. She had to pull out of school during the second semester of her freshman year.

I wanted to be a good dad. I wanted to be a better father than mine was to me. I wanted to be the man he wasn't. I promised myself that I would love my kid in ways that Joe never loved me. My kids would look at me and smile, knowing that they had a good father. They would be proud to call me Dad.

On August 8, 1998, our daughter was born at St. John's Hospital. She was an angel to me from the first time I held her in my arms. I couldn't believe how big her brown eyes were. Liza had always loved the name Destiny and I felt that it was fitting. We gave her the middle name Catherine to honor my mother.

As Destiny came into the world, I was heading into my first official season of college basketball, and there was a lot of hype.

Folks in Rhode Island weren't used to it, but it followed me everywhere, so it felt normal. The media attention expanded exponentially. Rhode Island was ranked in the top twenty-five in the AP preseason poll. *Sports Illustrated* came to town and wrote a lengthy story. Everything was going well . . . until it wasn't.

The first game of the season, I started out on fire, racking up twenty-five points, eleven rebounds, and ten assists. But that's not what I remember about that game.

In our first matchup, and I'm not sure what possessed me, I wore a pair of Nike Air Jordans during a nationally televised game on ESPN. After a quick start, we were featured in a magazine spread with an action shot of me swooping to the hoop with the Jordan insignia on the bottom of the shoe displayed prominently for the camera.

Sonny nearly lost his mind. In the world of sneaker branding, there was no bigger offense. To Sonny, this was worse than getting caught with a prostitute. This was treason. Now Sonny had to go back and explain to his Adidas bosses. Sonny and Gary grilled me for days afterward.

"What were you thinking?" demanded Sonny. "Do you know how bad this looks?"

As usual, I wasn't too worried about it. Plus, Sonny could never stay mad at me for long.

Shortly after that, we had a quick break from classes, and I decided to head down to New York. I jumped on the train and Liza surprised me by meeting me at Penn Station. I had been a swirl of emotions and wanted to talk to her. My mother was never far from my mind, and depending on the day, the sadness of her memory could hit me like a flash flood.

We got something to eat and then headed to Grandma Mildred's house, where I opened up to Liza. Everything came rushing out. I cried and I told her how hard it was to struggle daily with the loss of my mom. Things were happening fast in my life, and I really wanted Mom to be there for me. And not only did I miss her, but there was almost no one to talk to about her. As an only child, I had no one else to shoulder the burden. I had to do it alone, and sometimes it got so heavy I couldn't carry it. I found out that day that Liza could carry some of it for me, and that night we talked about it for the first time.

After an up-and-down season, we sat at 19–12 heading into what would be a surprise run through the Atlantic 10 Tournament. I had a terrific year with averages of 17.6 points, 9.4 rebounds, and 3.8 assists on 48 percent field-goal shooting. Although I was open to staying at Rhode Island for another season, my name was being bounced around as the possible number-one overall pick if I declared for the NBA draft.

Several hours before the Atlantic 10 title game, Gary called and wanted me to meet with Sonny at his suite. Once I arrived, Sonny and Gary introduced me to a man I'd never met before.

"Meet Dan Fegan," said Sonny. "He's your new agent."

I thought to myself: *That ain't my agent.*

I can't say for sure what happened, but when universities and corporate interests are involved, deals will be made. Gary was a power broker. Once again, I was being bought and sold.

Gary vehemently denied it. I didn't realize that a lot of relationships were about to go off the rails. This was where friendships forged over the years would be tested. I left the hotel suite without saying anything one way or the other, and once again, my head was filled with everything except what I was supposed to be concentrating on: the biggest game of my life in three hours. I took a quick nap to free my mind.

When we arrived at the old Spectrum arena in Philadelphia, my head was pretty clear. I was focused and had a great week of practice. The game was physically exhausting. In classic John Chaney fashion, Temple contested every basket with bruisers like future NBA player Mark Karcher and six-foot-ten DC native Kevin Lyde. Their zone was just as impregnable as it was frustrating. We hoisted one missed jumper after another because we just couldn't get into the paint.

The score was 59–59 when I ripped down a rebound from a long three with ten seconds to go. I advanced the ball to half court, and we called time-out with 6.1 seconds remaining. Coach Harrick tried to calm us down on the sideline. But it just felt like chaos. The moment was so big.

"This play is going to Junior," screamed Harrick.

That's what he called me. Junior. He kept screaming that Junior was getting the ball. He didn't have an actual play. Nothing was drawn up. I had missed my last four shots, but it didn't matter.

"Just get it to Junior," Harrick implored.

We inbounded the ball in front of Temple's bench. I was highly aware that there were just six precious seconds on the clock. As soon as I got the inbounds pass beyond half court,

I took off downcourt near the left sideline and tried to rock myself into a rhythm, realizing I had to get the shot up quickly.

It was just feeling where the sideline was. Anticipating where the three-point line was. My senses were on fire like never before. Then I looked up at the clock and just let the ball go. Not to be cocky, but under that type of immense pressure . . . I knew it was going in as soon as it left my hand.

I never heard the horn, but I saw the ball drop through the net. The place exploded. I turned and ran down to the other end of the floor. I think that was the fastest I'd ever run in my life. I fell to the floor in the corner of the opposite baseline. My teammates tackled me. I could hardly breathe. I started to cry. My teammate Antonio Reynolds-Dean wouldn't let me get up, trying to stretch the moment forever.

After the game I was drained. I sat at my locker with tears running down my face. I cried like a baby. Ten minutes later the sports information director told me it was time to go to the press conference.

"Just let him sit for a bit," Antonio said to the SID. "Let him get it all out."

It was the single best moment of my basketball career.

Outside the locker room everyone was waiting. Gary had a huge smile on his face. At least I was back to wearing Adidas, I'm sure he was thinking. I found Greg and embraced him.

"Hey, man, we're outta here," I said, letting him know that save for the NCAA Tournament, my time at Rhode Island was over.

"I got two more years of school left," Greg said. "My moms ain't letting me leave New York until I got my degree in hand."

"Nah, let's go. Wherever I go you have to come, too."

"We'll figure it out, Lamar."

That was good enough for me. Right then, life was good.

A week later Rhode Island lost to UNC Charlotte 80–71 in the first round of the NCAA Tournament. And just like that, my amateur career was over. I had gone back and forth about whether or not I wanted to stay in school or declare for the draft— my typical indecisiveness—but deep down I knew it was time.

I was ready for the next level.

After the season ended, I left Rhode Island and returned to New York. But New York isn't exactly the kind of place to escape to when everybody wants to know what your next move is. Things started happening quickly. There were many matters to deal with, including picking an agent, pre-draft workouts, and signing with a sneaker company. That's where Sonny would come back into the picture. After years of bringing me to his events, giving me advice, and wooing me at every turn, Sonny wanted to see a return on his investment. I had always known this day was coming, and I dreaded it.

Even though things between me and Sonny were rocky, he still desperately wanted to fix them. And it's not as if he wasn't riding high. He signed Kobe in the spring of 1996, and their hug at the NBA draft that June, caught on camera, signified a new era for Adidas basketball. The following year, Sonny landed his prized Tracy McGrady, giving him the two most exciting young players in all of basketball.

A few years before, Sonny had moved from Southern California to an apartment in New York City in order to be closer to Kobe. After Kobe was signed, sealed, and delivered, Sonny kept a room for me in his apartment on Madison Avenue near Central Park. His wife, Pam, would pack the pantry with sweets, including boxes of cheesecake, my favorite. I had a key to the apartment and could drop by whenever I wanted to get away. Pam would take me shopping and we'd go to the movies. It was almost like I was her son.

After the season, Sonny naturally wanted to talk to me about the series of huge decisions that lay ahead of me. Most importantly, whether or not I was going to follow in the footsteps of Kobe and Tracy and sign with Adidas.

Sonny takes his food very seriously. Oftentimes meetings, decisions, and deals revolved around food, particularly Italian food. Both Sonny and Pam were great cooks, so one day not long after the NCAA Tournament, Sonny arranged dinner at his house to talk about the future.

The spread was elaborate. There was pasta Bolognese, linguine, breaded chicken, eggplant, and salad with romaine lettuce, cucumbers, and tomatoes topped with balsamic vinegar. I mean the works. It rivaled New York City's finest Italian restaurant. Pam had started cooking three hours before I arrived.

When Gary and I showed up, Pam greeted us at the door. She always had such a warm smile and genuinely seemed to have a special affinity for me. Sonny reminded me often how much she loved me. The atmosphere was warm and friendly, but deep inside I could feel a tension growing. My stomach was in knots.

We sat down to eat, and the food was delicious. Sonny was to my right at the head of the table. Gary was to my left, and Pam sat across from me.

"Lamar, we been through a lot together," Sonny started. "I've seen you grow, mature, and learn. I've seen you become a man. I want to sign you to Adidas, and I want to be your personal manager."

"No," I said flatly without even considering it.

It seemed like time just stopped. They were clearly not expecting that response. I looked up at Pam and she was appalled. You would think "666" was scrawled on my forehead the way she looked at me. And I loved Pam. We really connected from the moment I met her, but at that table she looked right through me.

In their minds, this dinner was just a formality. All Sonny had to do was say the word and I'd fall in line as usual. I mean, I was just a kid from the hood who followed the money and lacked the ability to make important decisions for himself. Right?

Not this time.

It was Vegas. It had been nearly two years since I was dumped out in the desert with no one to call, and the hurt feelings were still warm in my veins. Over and over in my mind, I had played the day I got my dismissal letter and that following week. Now I was supposed to act like it never happened. A twelve-million-dollar offer was supposed to make me forget that Sonny, who surely knew about my dismissal before I did, never called me?

There in his dining room, for the first time, I stood up for what I believed. I was proud of myself. I held my ground. I would not be bought—not this time. I made *my* decision. I never wore a pair of Adidas again.

14

In April of 1999, two months before the NBA draft, I signed with agent Jeff Schwartz. The move raised a lot of eyebrows because at that point in his career, Jeff had very little experience dealing with NBA players. His major focus at the time was tennis. People scratched their heads and wondered why I would forgo bigger, more established names. The answer is that I had an instant rapport with Jeff, and he felt like the straightest shooter of the bunch. He was learning the NBA ropes, just as I was. I feel like I made the right decision because, to this day, he's the only agent I've ever had.

Jeff set me up with a Nike sneaker deal, and even though it was less than what I could have gotten at Adidas, I didn't mind because it's where I wanted to be. We soon organized workouts and interviews with NBA teams and tested my value in the draft. I was happy things were moving in the right direction and even more so to have legitimate money in my pocket. Money that wasn't under the table or passed through some shady back channel. It was money that I earned.

But having that money opened up a whole new world for me and divided my attention when I was supposed to be focused on the draft. All of a sudden, I had the most freedom I'd ever experienced in my life. Man, I wanted to have some fun.

The Chicago Bulls had the number-one pick in the draft and they wanted me. My dream of making it to the NBA was so close it almost didn't feel real. It was both a stressful and exciting time as well as exhilarating and intoxicating. I was the center of attention, and new people were coming into my life left and right. There was nothing but opportunity in front of me.

The 1999 NBA draft was on the last Thursday of June and would take place in Washington, DC, at what was then the MCI Center, the home of the Washington Wizards.

The weekend before the draft, with most of my draft workouts out of the way, I wanted to blow off a little steam and hit Greekfest on Jones Beach, Long Island. Greekfest is one of the largest annual gatherings for young black people on the East Coast and attracts black fraternities, sororities, athletes, celebrities, and seemingly half of New York to party and hook up on the beach.

However, I was due to head to Chicago the next morning to work out for the Bulls top brass. They were sending a chartered jet for me to Teterboro Airport in New Jersey, which is the preferred airport for private jets in the tristate area.

Greg called me Friday night to make sure I was ready to show the Bulls what I was all about. Kill the workout and I'd be the face of the franchise. I could start an era that picked up where Michael Jordan left off. What a dream.

"You ready to go?" Greg asked. "I'm gonna pick you up at nine in the morning to head to the airport."

Bulls general manager Jerry Krause and head coach Tim Floyd would make the trip in that private jet to pick me up, and we'd do the interview on the two hour and forty-five-minute flight to Chicago. Then I'd work out at the practice facility as soon as we arrived.

About half an hour after Greg's call, I called him back and told him the workout was canceled. He didn't think anything of it. Happens all the time. Plus, we were new to the NBA and he didn't know better.

"Come pick me up anyway," I said. "We're going to Greekfest."

The next morning, we went to Greekfest and it was a blast. We were drinking, smoking, and meeting girls every ten steps we took. I had at least $10,000 in my pocket. I felt like a star because everybody knew me. In five days I'd be in the NBA. I felt great. *This is the life,* I thought.

Right in the middle of all the fun, sometime around 4 PM, Greg saw that he had about a dozen missed calls on his cell phone. Now you have to understand, this was the late 1990s and people didn't check their phone every thirty seconds. Greg listened to the first message. It was Gary, and man, was he pissed. He was yelling so loud on the message we could barely make it out because of all the distortion.

"Where the fuck are you guys?" screamed Gary. "They've been waiting for six hours!"

"They" were Jerry Krause and Tim Floyd. They were waiting at the airport, just sitting on the plane, calling whoever they could to get ahold of us.

The truth is I lied. The workout wasn't canceled. I didn't want to go. I didn't want to be a Bull.

Looking back, I feel like I simply didn't want the pressure or the responsibility. That was a damn bright spotlight. I believed in my abilities, and I've always stood out, but I like being in a situation where I share the load with my teammates. I didn't want an entire franchise to rely on me. Or put their hopes in me. To be honest, I don't know. I just knew I didn't want to play for Chicago. Not even if it meant going down in history as the number-one overall pick.

The Vancouver Grizzlies had the second pick, and I didn't want that either. They could have had Michael Jordan and Scottie Pippen, and I still wouldn't have wanted to go there. I had Greg call Grizzlies general manager Stu Jackson the day after Greekfest and tell him we weren't going to Vancouver and not to draft me. Greg was nineteen and had zero experience in dealing with agents or front-office people who didn't want to talk to him in the first place. He was a sophomore guard at St. Francis University in New York, juggling a full course load. He wasn't Jerry Maguire.

Meanwhile, Stu Jackson was the general manager of a franchise struggling to find a foothold. I could tell by the look on Greg's face that he didn't want to make that call. But neither did I. So he dialed the number.

"Excuse me, Mr. Jackson, this is a friend of Lamar Odom," Greg started with an unsure, shaky voice. "He just wanted to let you know that he doesn't want you to draft him. He's not going to be happy in Vancouver. You know the knock on him is that he's a little unstable. I just wanted to make sure there wasn't any confusion."

There was a pause on the line before Jackson replied.

"Who the fuck are you?" Jackson asked, none too pleased. Greg handed the phone back to me.

"You talk to him," he said. I just hung up the phone. That took care of Vancouver.

The Charlotte Hornets wanted a guard with the third pick so they were going to take Steve Francis or Baron Davis, whoever was available.

It was draft night, and the Clippers were on the clock. The phones were buzzing like crazy. Jeff Schwartz had been working the lines with several different teams all day. But I did not want to go to the Clippers. Anywhere but the Clippers. They were perennially the worst franchise in the NBA. The league's doormat. Last in everything, including respectability. But I was running out of options because I wasn't going to last very long on the draft board.

Jeff picked up the phone for the last time before the selection would be announced. It was Clippers general manager Elgin Baylor telling him that they were taking me with the fourth pick.

I was officially a franchise savior.

Welcome to the NBA, Lamar.

I had taken care of all my loose ends in New York, and everything was set up in Los Angeles. I was about to start the journey of a lifetime. But there was one last thing I had to do. Or, I should say, one thing Liza wanted me to do: visit my mother.

It had been seven years since my mother died, and I had never been to her grave. The thought of visiting the cemetery was just too much for me.

"I don't think I'll be able to handle it," I said.

"You have to go," said Liza. "To say goodbye. For her. And for you."

So, we all went. My grandmother, Aunt JaNean, Liza, and several cousins. When we got there, I could feel anxiety and nervousness coursing through my body. I had never gotten any kind of therapy or help for my mental state. Her passing led directly to the larger problems I had as an adult, and I've never been eager to confront them, despite knowing the root causes.

But there at that cemetery was a chance for me to start. My eyes welled up as everyone gave me a moment to be alone with my mom. I could feel my hands sweating and my chest tightening. It didn't seem real that my mother was right there. I was this close to Mommy. I tried not to think about the pain and to instead remember the good times and the things she taught me. I wondered how proud she would be if she could see where I was going.

What would she think of me? Did I turn out the way she thought I would? Was I the man she thought I'd be? What would she say to me? What would I say to her?

I laid down a number 7 Clippers jersey on her grave. I wiped the tears from my eyes and said goodbye to Cathy Celestine Odom.

Liza was thrilled that I had finally achieved my dream, but the moment was bittersweet for her. She wasn't exactly thrilled about me going to Los Angeles; New York would always be her home. Plus, lurid stories about all the beautiful women, temptations, and glitzy parties were not in short supply, and she knew me all too well. She didn't relish the idea of me being within arm's reach of so many willing and eager young ladies. So we needed to plot out our future.

"I want us to be a family," I told her as we sat on the couch in her mother's living room. "I want us to be together. It wouldn't be LA without you."

Knowing that I wanted her in my life and close to me allayed some of her fears. Right away I started to make preparations for the big move to Los Angeles. We got a three-bedroom condo in a towering glass building in Marina del Rey, which was a popular spot with a lot of guys on the team. We were right on the water in a trendy neighborhood. All you had to do to get to the Staples Center was jump on Washington Boulevard for the twenty-minute drive.

Liza was excited for this adventure, but it was difficult for her to get adjusted to her new life. Neither one of us had a driver's license, which made getting around tough. My friend Alex Harris drove me to practices and games, but when I was away, Liza was stuck at home. She was nineteen with a baby and no social circle. I hired a driver so she could get out of the house. That gave her a little more freedom, but it wasn't enough. There was no getting around the fact that she didn't have any friends, and it was difficult for her to meet people. She made friends with my teammate Maurice Taylor's girlfriend and future wife, Tiffany, who helped her navigate her new world. But Liza needed more.

I offered to fly her cousin Kevin, who she was really close with, to LA, so at least she'd have some company when I'd be gone on long road trips. That made things a little easier for her, and Liza began to settle into a comfortable routine.

Shortly after, my first NBA training camp rolled around, and I was as excited as anyone to get started. As was normally the case with me, I played very little basketball over the summer. Factoring in moving to a new city and tying up loose ends in an old one, I rarely had time to step on the court, but I was still in really good shape.

When I arrived at my first practice, I was not impressed with what I saw. Back then the Clippers practiced at Southwest College, a community college not far from South Central, while classes were in session. Students would peek through the double doors of the gym while we worked on defensive rotations or ran sprints.

When it got hot in the gym, we propped open the back door with a cinder block. There was no security. Anyone could walk in, and they often did. There wasn't even a place to shower. We had to drive home in our sweaty practice gear. If someone needed some muscle work, a trainer propped up a massage table at the end of the court.

The facilities were the worst in the league, and part of the reason the Clippers were a laughingstock had to do with the tight-fisted owner, Donald Sterling. The facilities were barely suitable for a junior college team, let alone an NBA franchise.

I had envisioned everything in the NBA being top-notch, so this didn't come close to matching my hopes. Hell, we had better facilities at Rhode Island. It didn't exactly inspire confidence or project a championship attitude, but titles were a long way off with or without the amenities. The Clippers hadn't even been to the playoffs since 1993 or won a playoff series since 1976.

We were projected to finish at the bottom of the Pacific Division, which was not surprising since our team was a collection of journeyman veterans and players even avid fans had never heard of. We were a decent bunch of guys, but it was a hodgepodge of players just thrown together.

Our first game was November 2, 1999, at the brand-spanking-new Staples Center. I remember everything being so clean. It was the opposite of where we practiced. When I walked into our locker room and saw my jersey hanging in my locker, I stopped in my tracks. I was finally here.

When I slipped the jersey over my head, I walked over to a mirror and stared. It hit me that all my hard work, all the pain, all the sacrifice had led me directly to this exact moment standing in front of this mirror. There I was, looking back at me. I smiled because there was one inescapable fact.

"I'm in the NBA," I said out loud.

My debut couldn't have gone better. I might as well have been at Lincoln Park. No one could guard me. I was smooth with the ball, and no one knew how to play me. They were confused by a six-foot-ten, left-handed point forward who could dribble like a guard and played with crazy swagger. We opened against the Seattle Supersonics and their two stars, Vin Baker and Horace Grant, had no idea what to do about me. They had guarded near the basket their entire careers and looked afraid to step out to the perimeter to check me.

I sliced them up for thirty points, twelve rebounds, three assists, two blocks, and two steals. The Clippers looked like geniuses for picking me. It was just one game, but I came off like the franchise-saving superstar everyone imagined I would be. I thought: *This is going to be easy. I'm going to tear this league apart.*

Things took off from there as I scored double figures in my first nineteen games and won NBA Rookie of the Month for November. After every game, the star from the other team would stop me with praise. The same, however, couldn't be said about the Clippers. We started the season 4–16, including a crushing nine-game losing streak in December. Things never got better, and after falling to 11–34, head coach Chris Ford was fired. We were second to last in points scored and points allowed. Not a winning combination. The Clippers were also second to last in attendance. Some nights you could hear people talking on the concourse level while the game was in progress. We finished the season with the worst record in the league at 15–67.

But I was really satisfied with my rookie year. I made First Team All-Rookie with averages of 16.6 points, 7.8 rebounds, 4.2 assists, 1.3 blocks, and 1.2 steals, delivering on my promise in a big way. I felt like the sky was the limit. If I didn't win MVP someday, it would be my own fault. I was thinking big.

15

For my second year with the Clippers, I rented a house in the exclusive Strand neighborhood along the canals in Marina del Rey. Liza had had enough of life in Los Angeles and returned to New York. She wanted to finish school as well as be close to family who could help with Destiny. I had told her back when we were kids that I was going to marry her someday, but we never did get married. Our rocky on-again, off-again relationship suffered for many reasons, my infidelity included, but throughout it all, even when we weren't together, we remained close and parented as a team.

With Liza back home, I had two of my friends from New York move out with me, Alex Harris, who had played football at Bowie State, and Kamal McQueen, a former high school teammate at Christ the King who we all called Mally.

Going into the 2000–01 season, I felt like I was getting my bearings, and things were about to take off. Jerry DeGregorio had finished his first season as Rhode Island's head coach when Jeff Schwartz called the Clippers looking for a job for Jerry. He was quickly hired as a player development coach and moved to Los Angeles. Everyone thought it was a good idea that Jerry was close so that he could look after me. Greg still had one year of school and wouldn't move out until the following year.

My new house became a playground for me and my friends. There was a revolving door of women week in and week out. With Liza back in New York, it was so much easier to meet other women, and I was *down* to meet women. Lots of them. And even though I was being drug tested for the first time in my life, it didn't stop me from smoking weed throughout most of the season.

I was so excited with my new life. I had never expected to be in this position. I'd walk out my front door and marvel at the fact that I lived in this fancy neighborhood and had come so far from Queens.

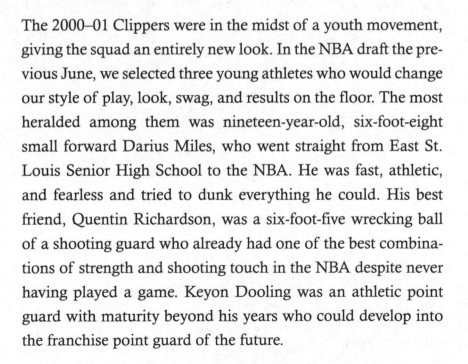

The 2000–01 Clippers were in the midst of a youth movement, giving the squad an entirely new look. In the NBA draft the previous June, we selected three young athletes who would change our style of play, look, swag, and results on the floor. The most heralded among them was nineteen-year-old, six-foot-eight small forward Darius Miles, who went straight from East St. Louis Senior High School to the NBA. He was fast, athletic, and fearless and tried to dunk everything he could. His best friend, Quentin Richardson, was a six-foot-five wrecking ball of a shooting guard who already had one of the best combinations of strength and shooting touch in the NBA despite never having played a game. Keyon Dooling was an athletic point guard with maturity beyond his years who could develop into the franchise point guard of the future.

Like me, they were all twenty years of age or younger, and overnight we became the NBA's most exciting team. We were fun and full of so much promise. We were so young that people jokingly referred to us as the best AAU team ever. We pushed the ball whenever we could, resulting in as many turnovers as highlight plays. It elevated my game to run alongside the young guns. I could make the kind of plays distributing the ball I couldn't with the previous year's team. I was so happy with the influx of youth and how well everyone bonded and got along with one another. We were just the coolest bunch of kids in the NBA, and we knew it.

My numbers jumped up across the board to 17.2 points, 7.9 rebounds, 5.4 assists, and 46 percent field-goal shooting. Unfortunately, my numbers weren't the only thing that increased. I was smoking marijuana more regularly. It was everywhere—in my pockets, my car, my house. I thought I could anticipate the random drug tests, but I couldn't.

I failed a drug test in the spring of 2001 and was suspended for five games in March. I really felt like I let people down. For the first time, my pot smoking affected someone other than me. Trust me, I did not feel good about that. Although head coach Alvin Gentry was disappointed, he and the team were very supportive.

When I addressed the media, I said:

This will definitely not happen again. The fans have been great to me since I've been here, and I hope it continues. I hope everyone doesn't pass judgment on my mistake. I've made a couple and I may make a couple again, but hopefully they won't be as big as this one.

People believed me, but the words felt hollow. I used the phrase "my mistake," but it wasn't a mistake. It was a habit. A lifestyle. I was surprised it actually took this long for someone to catch me, but I knew I wasn't going to stop. I just figured I had to be more careful or at least wait until the summer when there would be no random tests. While I was suspended, I took part in an aftercare program, but I didn't take it seriously and eventually stopped doing it.

The Clippers improved to 31–51 that year—sixteen more wins than my rookie season—and even though we failed to make the playoffs, we were headed in the right direction.

Going into the 2001–02 season, my third year, the buzz around Clippers basketball had reached a fever pitch. We acquired my former Riverside AAU teammate Elton Brand and were predicted to win forty games and have a real shot at the play-offs for the first time in ten years. The number of season ticket sales skyrocketed to a record 12,000. The sellout opening night crowd was a Clipper record 19,445. In some ways we were getting more buzz than the Lakers.

Then three games into the season the bottom fell out. I failed my second drug test in eight months and was suspended for another five games. This time support did not flow from every corner of the franchise like it had the first time. People were angry, disgusted, and fed up. Their faith in me was waning, and for the first time, my future with the franchise was in doubt.

"I am very disappointed," Elgin Baylor, the Clippers general manager, said in a written statement. "Lamar has let his teammates down as well as our entire organization."

"It's ridiculous that it's happened," added Coach Gentry. "We're very disappointed. I don't think mad is the right word. I'm more disappointed."

I was down. I mean I was hurting and embarrassed by my lack of professionalism. The day after my twenty-second birthday, I delivered a tearful press conference. I was more disappointed in myself than Coach Gentry ever could have been.

"This time you can trust me," I told my coaches and teammates. It would not be the last time I used that line. I didn't give much thought to the aftercare program I was required to go through. I rarely even showed up. No one questioned me about it, so I wasn't worried.

Along with the five-game suspension, a bruised foot and sore shoulder held me to just twenty-six games and a career low 13.1 points per game on an inefficient 41 percent from the field.

The only highlight of that time of my life was the birth of my and Liza's son on January 1, 2002. We named him Lamar Jr.

16

In the spring of 2002, Greg's senior season at St. Francis had ended, and he was eager to join me in LA. It was the tail end of my unspectacular third season with the Clippers that had been limited to less than thirty games. Despite the fact that my agent, Jeff Schwartz, and longtime mentor Jerry DeGregorio were living in Los Angeles, most everyone felt that ultimately things would be best if Greg moved in with me and resumed his role of looking out for my interests.

But before I could even talk to Greg, he was on a plane to Los Angeles. The ticket was paid for by agent Dan Fegan, who was using Greg in a last-ditch effort to win me over. Greg was willing to help, but couldn't tell anyone what he was doing. The whole thing was Gary and Dan's ploy.

Gary was still Fegan's guy and felt like he could make things right by finally delivering me to him. There were still a lot of hurt feelings from what went down before the draft, but Greg wanted to do what he could to relieve some of the long-simmering tension. Of course, this wasn't going to make Jeff very happy. And as usual, I wanted to do what I could to avoid conflict.

It was the last game of the season, and Greg had just arrived in LA. I hadn't even spoken to him. Greg headed straight to the

game, but I wasn't there. Greg spotted Jerry DeGregorio walking off the floor after the game.

"JD!" called Greg.

"What are you doing here?" asked a stunned Jerry.

Greg might as well have been the Angel of Death. He
couldn't possibly tell Jerry why he was in town.

"I'm here to see Lamar."

"Lamar's not here. I'll take you to his house."

So, they jumped in Jerry's car and headed over to my place
in the Marina.

Greg walked in the front door and I was stunned to see
him. The next day, we went to lunch at Jerry's Deli in West-
wood. I ordered a couple BLT sandwiches, a plate of chicken
tenders, and a giant strawberry milkshake, and he filled me in
on the nature of his surprise visit.

"Dan and Gary are out here," he said. "They want to talk. I
don't know if you want to fuck with them but you at least gotta
sit with them."

We drove to Greg's hotel to pick up his stuff so he could
move in with me. In the meantime, he called Fegan, who
picked up the phone immediately.

"Lamar's ready to talk," said Greg. "Where should we
meet you at?"

"I'm at a family barbecue," replied Fegan. "I'll call you in
a day."

We were stunned. He didn't want to meet? I was ready
now. He flew Greg out, came up with this grand plan, and then
showed no urgency.

"Fuck him. I'm not meeting," I said.

I couldn't believe he would waste our time like that. I never talked to him again. Greg stayed in Los Angeles and partied with me until June. Then we picked up and flew back to New York. And for the rest of the summer, I slept on the pleather couch in Greg's two-bedroom apartment, which was a fourth-floor walkup in the Brownsville section of Brooklyn. This was the straight-up hood, but it was cool to be back home. The only alteration I made to the apartment was to buy a new air conditioner that we set up on the windowsill.

Living in a big house in a ritzy, celebrity-filled neighborhood mere steps from the Pacific Ocean, I'd almost forgotten what it was like to be a native New Yorker. So, we just got back to our roots. When I wasn't visiting Liza and the kids, I sat on the steps in front of Greg's building and flirted with the girls who walked by. People offered to cook for me, and I slipped them a couple racks to go buy groceries. I got to know everyone on the block, from shorties riding bikes and old heads dispensing knowledge, to street vendors who served up onion-smothered hot dogs, barbecue, and Italian ices.

I had money in my pocket and people who loved to be around me. I moved freely on the block. This is how we lived . . . and it was bliss.

In the late summer of 2002, when the sweltering but relaxing Brooklyn days began to fade away, we started making arrangements to head back to Los Angeles for my fourth season with the Clippers. Greg agreed to move to LA and be my manager.

It would be his first season with me full-time as a pro and our first basketball season under the same roof since Redemption Christian six years ago.

While Greg liked to have fun and enjoyed the jet-set life-style, he was far more hardnosed than my other friends when it came to our careers. After all, Greg was now on board in an official capacity and had dreams of managing a stable of ath-letes or possibly becoming an agent. When he moved in with me, he cleaned house and helped me redo my entire program. That meant jettisoning some of the people who had been with me since my rookie season.

Greg knew Kamal McQueen from the basketball circuit, but he wasn't all that familiar with Al Harris and the rest of my friends. Greg moved them to apartments in Sherman Oaks, forty-five minutes from my house. They were not happy about it, but they got free apartments and had their own space, so they didn't have much room to complain. There were also sev-eral new rules put in place. No one was allowed to smoke in my cars. In fact, Greg didn't allow drugs of any kind near anything registered in my name. After I'd been suspended twice for vio-lating the NBA's drug policy, Greg knew that something had to change. The environment I created was too lax. My house was party central, and there seemed to be marijuana smoke wafting through the crib at every hour of the day.

But this season had to be different: it was my contract year. The following summer I would become a restricted free agent and be able to sign my first veteran deal. There were tens of millions of dollars on the line. A third drug suspension would kill all of that and have me on a rail heading straight out of the league and back to Queens permanently.

Greg and I moved from our old house on the Strand to another: a new four-bedroom house in the Marina about ten minutes away. Our new setup included Greg, me, and Gus "Gusto" Kennedy, who had at one time managed the Long Island Panthers. Our new house was on Westwind Street along the Ballona Lagoon and was one of the most picturesque neighborhoods in LA. Harrison Ford lived two doors down. Directly across the street was a two-story villa Jean-Claude Van Damme called home. Every morning he'd step out on his balcony in his briefs, flex his ripped torso, and do yoga.

By the time the season rolled around, I felt focused and recharged. I locked in. I wasn't gonna smoke. I was going to eat right. I was going to do everything my coaches asked of me. But mostly, I was going to play the best basketball of my career. No one had more at stake than I did. If I slipped back into my harmful ways and jeopardized my career, it would be no one's fault but my own.

Greg also took over as my full-time driver, and as my top lieutenant, he came to every game—home and away—that season. He stayed at team hotels and arranged dozens of flights to make it to each city to be there with me before and after the game.

"I have to watch you twenty-four seven so you don't fuck this up," he'd say.

He even drove me to and from every practice that year.

Despite all of the team's promise and no matter how locked-in I felt, we were going backward. After the All-Star break, Coach Gentry was struggling. The life had gone from his eyes. He was listless as he drew up plays that he knew we were probably not going to execute properly. As it looked like we'd miss the playoffs yet again, the players started to tune him out. Clippers vice president Elgin Baylor had lost faith in him, and they were barely speaking. The wheels had come off, and the players started thinking about vacation plans. We had blown twenty leads in the fourth quarter—more than any team in the league. We couldn't guard anybody. We were getting booed at home. It felt like the team, despite its young core, was about to be blown up.

On March 3, 2003, word came down from the front office: Gentry was out. We were 19–39, last in the Pacific Division and riding a six-game losing streak. In three years with the Clips, Gentry had an 89–133 record. That was it.

"These decisions are never easy, and this one is especially tough, because Alvin and I had a very good working relationship," Baylor told the *New York Times*.

On a road trip late in the season, I ran into an old face. After the game, waiting in the hallway outside the visitors' locker room of the United Center in Chicago was Sonny Vaccaro. I was stunned to see him since we hadn't crossed paths in years. The look on his face was one I'd never seen before. He wasn't beaming or boasting. He didn't greet me with one of his hearty, raspy-voiced hellos. His eyes looked sad. His demeanor was reserved. We exchanged warm pleasantries, but not enough to thaw any of the hurt between us.

I don't hate Sonny. I don't even dislike him. I respect Sonny. In many ways I still love him. We had been through so much together, but I won't ever forget that summer in Las Vegas.

After several moments, Sonny's eyes began to well up. Then tears streamed down his face. He tried to force words but couldn't speak. He grabbed me by the face and kissed me on the cheek. It was an old-school Italian thing. It caught me off guard, but I didn't protest. I'm a young black guy from the hood, and kissing another man is not part of our culture. But it was his way of saying he loved me after all this time.

I hugged Sonny and we parted without a word.

The season was a loss, and I battled lingering injuries. I played just forty-nine games, bringing my past two-year total to seventy-eight.

I finished the season averaging 14.6 points, 6.7 rebounds, and 3.6 assists on 43 percent shooting from the field. More importantly, I didn't fail any drug tests. I felt I had played well enough to warrant a big contract in the off-season and was looking forward to sitting down at the negotiating table and setting myself up for life.

Boy, was I in for a surprise.

17

With free agent negotiations looming, I was both nervous and excited. I was in for the biggest payday of my life. Real NBA money. The rocky seasons were in the rearview mirror, and I'd proven my worth as one of the most versatile young players in the league.

In June, after my fourth season with the Clippers, Greg, Al Harris, and I were out in Hollywood for a little fun. Nothing big, just blowing off steam. On the drive home, about a mile from my house, my phone rang. It was a New York number. It was late in New York, but I didn't worry because I was used to people calling me at all hours. But on the other end was my Aunt JaNean. She didn't mince words.

"Lamar," she said, "your grandmother has died. You need to come home."

It was a shock, even though Grandma Mildred was in her eighth decade. It didn't hit me like a brick . . . more like a fog that hung over me and settled in slowly.

"What happened?" asked Greg.

"My grandmother passed away," I said, my voice cracking.

The guys fell quiet. Greg turned off the radio. We just sat there at a red light near my home like the world had stopped. When we pulled into the garage at the house several minutes later, I stayed in the car while they went inside. I sat by myself for more than an hour. I didn't cry. My tears would come in the days and weeks ahead. I just thought about her life and what she had given me.

All those years ago, she moved to New York from a sharecropper's town in Georgia to find a better life. I believe she did. She bought her very own house on 131st Street. Met and married the only man she'd ever loved. Had three daughters, one of them my mother. She gave me my personality and taught me what it was like to be a man and how to love someone more than you love yourself.

I sat in the car. I didn't ask why. Never questioned God.

I wore number 7 because it was her lucky number.

Mildred Mercer was eighty.

On July 12, 2003, the Clippers held a press conference announcing the hiring of veteran head coach Mike Dunleavy, who had had stints with the Lakers, Blazers, and Bucks. Meanwhile, I had just arrived in Miami to play in Zo's Summer Groove, Alonzo Mourning's charity basketball game.

When we returned to Los Angeles a week later, Greg and I met Dunleavy at the Ritz-Carlton in Marina del Rey. Dunleavy was going to make his initial offer. My agent, Jeff Schwartz, was still on his way to Los Angeles, so Greg and I went alone.

"Don't be surprised if it's not what you think it's going to be," Jeff had cautioned me. "They're going to start low. Just hear what they have to say."

Dunleavy quickly got down to business. It was up to Dunleavy, who was given a role in management decisions as well as his coaching duties, to build a winning team. I could tell he was loving the power. He had this cockiness that caught me off guard.

"We're prepared to offer you three years and twenty-four million dollars," said Dunleavy. "That's the most I can do."

That was not even one-third of what I felt my market value was, and it wasn't anything close to a max offer. The Nuggets had just offered our shooting guard Corey Maggette $42 million, and he had put up similar numbers to mine. The Clippers matched the offer without thinking about it.

But more importantly, Elton Brand, our leading scorer and rebounder, was the team's top priority, and Miami was looking for a cornerstone big who could play power forward and center, so they offered him a six-year, $84 million deal. If the Clippers didn't match the offer, it all but paved the way for me to return to LA. But we'd have to get those numbers up, and Dunleavy wasn't playing ball.

Greg and I just looked at each other, stunned. What the fuck was this? It was clear from the jump that I was not a high priority to Dunleavy. I stood up right after hearing the offer.

"Thanks for nothing," I said to him. I knew for a fact I was not taking that offer. That was the last time I ever spoke to Dunleavy.

The Clippers matched Brand's deal. Elton was on the beach in Miami, sitting on the sand with his toes in the water when he got the call.

Then I had a stroke of luck, thanks to another agent, Bill Duffy. Anthony Carter, the Heat's fifth-year point guard, was planning to pick up a $4.1 million player option on the final year of his contract; however, Duffy sent in the paperwork several minutes after the midnight deadline, making Carter a free agent. The Heat were overjoyed and immediately chose not to re-sign him.

They used the additional money to offer me a five-year, $63 million contract. The Clippers had fifteen days to match. They did not . . . largely because the deal that Jeff Schwartz and Heat coach Pat Riley cooked up included a $15 million signing bonus, which Riley gave me on the spot in his office.

I had gotten everything I wanted. I knew after the Dunleavy meeting that I had to leave the Clippers for a fresh start, and it had always been my dream to play for Pat Riley, who was my favorite coach. He was fond of saying I could be the next Magic Johnson, and he was ecstatic about pairing me with his new rookie, Dwyane Wade, who had superstar written all over him.

My happiness didn't prevent the Clippers from delivering a parting shot when we split.

"In the final analysis, the decision was based on issues of character and other risks involved," Elgin Baylor said in a statement released by the Clippers. It just confirmed my feeling that I was doing the right thing by leaving the Clippers.

A few days later, Greg, Jeff, and I flew to Miami for the official contract signing and press conference. The night we arrived, we went out to a club in South Beach. Even Jeff went along, and that wasn't usually his thing.

The press conference was set for 3 PM the next day, so I had Greg call my financial advisor to have a private jet ready for 6 PM so we could head back to LA and celebrate after addressing the media. I'd get my money, say a few words, and then get out clean.

We got to Riley's office around noon. It was meticulous and full of things that displayed his worldliness and appreciation of culture and the arts. He even had books on African culture. Just before we sat down, he turned to me.

"Is this your whole crew?" he asked, looking over at Greg, Jeff, and my trainer, Robbie Davis. "I need to know who's who."

"This is us," I replied.

Riley paused as if to feel me out. The look on his face said, "You better be telling the truth." Right away I knew I wasn't in Clipper Land anymore.

"You want a soda?" he asked me.

"No thank you," I replied.

"*You want a soda?*" he repeated, only more firmly, without so much as blinking.

"Okay, I'll take a Pepsi," I said quickly.

It was a test. He wanted to gauge my reaction. See if I had solid convictions and could make a simple, quick decision. Or maybe he just thought I was thirsty. *Was it about the soda?* I wondered later on. I was still trying to feel him out, too.

From there, he began to break down Miami Heat culture and what was expected of every man who put on the uniform.

It was the beginning of my indoctrination to the world of Pat Riley.

He wanted me to change out of my street clothes and get dressed in their brand-new practice uniforms for the press conference. When I got out to the practice court, I was surprised to see three of my new teammates, Caron Butler, Eddie Jones, and Brian Grant, dressed in practice gear and shooting around. Riley wanted as many members of the team as possible present to promote a family-like culture. He sat down and got the press conference started with a few opening remarks.

It's been a long summer, but a good summer. We were very fortunate to draft Dwyane Wade. In July, I was over with [Heat owner] Mr. Arison in the Mediterranean, and then I went to Hawaii with my wife and family. And I've been to seven Bruce Springsteen concerts. So that's been my summer. Today is the best day of all of them.

So, without any further ado, I would like to introduce a player I have a lot of respect for from a basketball standpoint. He is a talented player and has overcome some things that we all know about and are behind him and one of the reasons why we didn't talk much about those things is because we believe they are behind. I've been around basketball for about thirty-seven years, and there's only been one other player that I've coached that has ever had this much versatility as a player and able to play four different positions. That player was Magic Johnson . . . So I want to introduce the newest member of the Miami Heat as we move on into the millennium: Lamar Odom.

After the press conference, we headed back to the locker room to get changed. I was feeling great that the formalities were out of the way and I could head back to Los Angeles for a bit.

"See you at seven AM tomorrow," Riley called out as we were leaving.

"Actually, I have a flight in an hour. I'll be back in a few weeks."

"No, I don't think you understand me," he replied. "We're working out tomorrow."

There was nothing I could say. He just gave me $15 million. I had to quickly get used to how things were going to be. And that meant early-morning workouts until Riley let me leave Miami. He was the boss now.

Riley taught me discipline. For all my gifts, I didn't have a clue about hard work and discipline. Pat loved my game but hated the way I went about the business of becoming a better basketball player. That was a hard pill for me to swallow. I wanted to be great, but I wasn't ready for the way Riley taught the game. When I arrived in Miami, I was a poodle. When I left I was a pit bull. It started the very moment he asked me if I wanted a soda.

I got set up for an indefinite stay at one of our favorite hotels, bought some clothes, and in between Riley's grueling workouts, learned the night scene.

One night we hit a club called Prive, which had three floors and was popular with celebrities and athletes. When we showed up, Eddie Jones and Brian Grant were already there. There were women everywhere. On the table in the booth were ten to fifteen $500 bottles of Louis Roederer Cristal champagne.

The bill came at four in the morning. The server set it on the table and Eddie picked it up and tossed it to me without even looking at it.

"Take care of that for me, young fella," he said as he got up to leave with his group.

I was afraid to look at it, but it wasn't going to pay itself. I opened the leather folder—$19,000. I was stunned. But I just ate it. I pulled out my American Express Black Card and reluctantly handed it over.

Two days later, I arrived at the arena for another workout, still miffed about getting stuck with such an exceptionally large bill. Sitting in my locker was an envelope containing a check for $15,000. Eddie walked out of the trainer's room with nothing on but his practice shorts. He looked at me with a huge grin. "Congratulations, you passed."

Welcome to Miami.

I thought I had found my true NBA home, and I needed a castle to call my own. After a quick search, I settled on a six-bedroom, nine-bathroom home in Pinecrest, Florida, which was about thirty miles from the arena and a twenty-minute jaunt from South Beach. It was perfect. Greg and I set up shop and outfitted it to be the perfect bachelor paradise.

We entertained often. Friends flew in from New York or Los Angeles, and I put them up in one of the extra bedrooms for as long as they wanted to stay. My favorite thing about my new crib was the backyard, which had a pool, Jacuzzi, and barbecue pit. The pool was where everything went down. To christen my new home, I invited about ten of my good friends over for a nighttime barbecue pool party. We worked the phones for a couple days, calling every stripper, groupie, and side piece we knew to come over around six. They were more than welcome to bring a friend or three.

All in all, there were about forty women there, and it didn't take long for half of them to get naked. It escalated quickly into a full-blown orgy. There's really no other way to describe it. People were having sex in the pool, the Jacuzzi, on the lawn, in chairs, standing up against a heat lamp. Everywhere. I met a pair of twenty-year-old twins who had zcro problcm with any request. For most of the night, I kept them to myself.

This was crazy, even for us. As the drugs and alcohol flowed, day disappeared into night, more girls arrived, and the party stretched into thc wcc hours, until every last fantasy had been fulfilled and every desire met.

Top left: My mother, Cathy Mercer, on her wedding day.

Top right: Mom and her sister JaNean, who looked out for me when Mom couldn't.

Bottom left: Wasn't I cute?

Bottom right: Surrounded by those I love best.

(Photos courtesy of JaNean Mercer)

Eighth grade graduation. *(Courtesy of JaNean Mercer)*

At right: Here I am dunking in high school. Love those old Nikes
I'm wearing. *(New York Daily News Archive/Contributor)*

Liza and I in 2000. My Terrell Davis jersey fit her
perfectly. *(Courtesy of Liza Morales)*

At right: Threading the needle. I wasn't a Rhode Island Ram for long, but I
was able to develop my game in my one playing year there. *(Rocky Widner)*

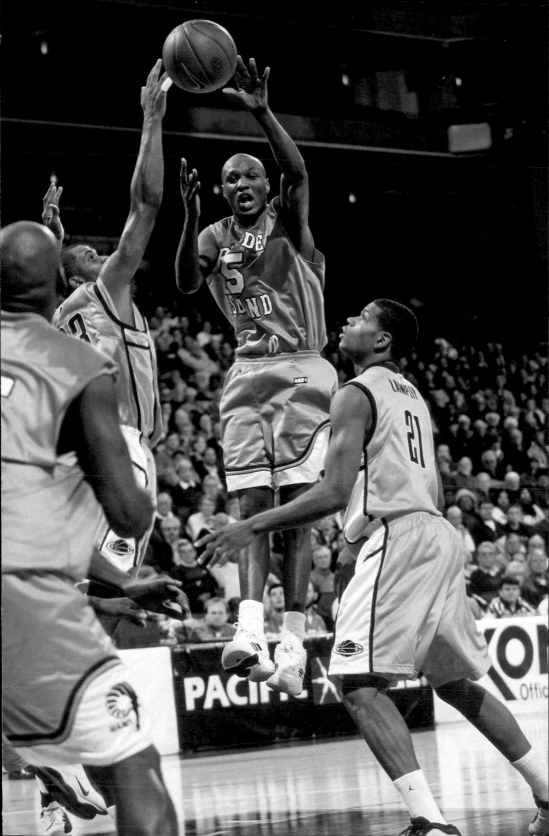

Top: LJ knows who's king!
(Courtesy of JaNean Mercer)

Bottom: Destiny and I take a well-deserved nap. *(Courtesy of Liza Morales)*

At right: Destiny and LJ with baby Jayden. *(Courtesy of JaNean Mercer)*

Draft night with the family. That's Grandma Mildred in
the red sweater. *(Courtesy of JaNean Mercer)*

At left: Shaking NBA Commissioner David Stern's hand during the
1999 Draft at the MCI Center in DC. *(Nathaniel S. Butler)*

Soft touch at the 2000 NBA Rookie Challenge Game at the
Oracle Arena in Oakland, CA. *(Andrew D. Bernstein)*

All love. I never had another teammate quite like Kobe Bryant. *(Stephen Dunn)*

Two kings from Queens. Ron Artest and me receiving our championship
rings before the start of the 2010 home opener. *(Gary Friedman)*

At right: Dunking against the Suns during Game Five of the
2010 NBA Western Conference Finals. *(Jeff Gross)*

At left: Always the center of attention. Kim, Khloe, and me in 2011, at the Hugo Bar for the launch of the Kardashian Handbag Kollection in Sydney, Australia. *(The Sydney Morning Herald)*

Top: Chip off the old block. My dad and me in 2008. *(Noel Vasquez/Contributor)*

Bottom: That smile. Sometimes it's all I got. *(Power Sports Images)*

The two lights of my life. *(Courtesy of JaNean Mercer)*

18

P at Riley never asked me directly about my past marijuana use. He hinted at it and demanded that it stay behind me ... that it would be unacceptable in his organization. I think he believed that I wouldn't let him down. Still, he insisted that whenever I went out at night, I be accompanied by a security guard of his choosing. That turned out to be the Heat's head of security, David Holcombe, a stocky, brooding, no-nonsense former cop who would later go on to be Dwyane Wade's personal security guard for nearly his entire career.

If I was planning to go out, I had to let Holcombe know, and he'd show up at my house or meet us out front of the club and shadow us the entire night. The next day he'd give Riley a full report of everything that went on. If I slipped up or didn't let him know about my plans, I'd get an earful from Riley the next day. On road trips, Holcombe always occupied the room next to mine.

Given that we went to strip clubs three nights a week, I'm not entirely sure what his reports consisted of. We'd often leave the club as the sun was coming up, with a couple strippers in tow. (It always surprised me to see the sun. Strip clubs don't have windows, so we never knew what time it was.) I'm guessing the reports didn't include the time a well-known young

NBA player, two years away from his first All-Star Game, was buck naked in a chair as a stripper gave him a lap dance.

"Put some damn clothes on," I told him. "You know how many people have been in that chair?"

If I was the voice of reason, you knew it was bad.

Preseason rolled around, and Riley's legendary three-hour practices were as tough as expected. Even though Stan Van Gundy was actually the head coach, this was still Riley's organization. He was responsible for putting it together and for any resulting success or failure. If you're not in great shape on day one, you're going to be in a considerable amount of pain. Guys were puking and gasping for air the first week, but Riley didn't care. He doesn't pay you to be average or out of shape.

I loved the culture and the camaraderie right away. The Heat offered the kind of structure and support I'd lacked so far in my NBA career. There was a great mix of talented, versatile veterans led by the smooth tenth-year swingman Eddie Jones and interior banger Brian Grant, who was a consummate professional and voice of reason in the locker room. Then there was the future of the franchise, the dynamic twenty-two-year-old rookie Dwyane Wade, who was billed as the player at the center of Miami's championship hopes. I had to find my role and was still uncertain when I should be a facilitator or an aggressor.

In the early fall of 2003, we were in Puerto Rico for a preseason game against the Sixers, and I really wanted to impress

Pat. If he told me to jump, I'd ask how high. If there was a brick wall, I would run through it. He talked to me every day about improving even the smallest detail of my game: from body language to taking a breath on the free-throw line. For Riley, there was no such thing as a detail too small. Since this was a preseason game, the starters were going to get big minutes in the first half and then sit the rest of the game. I wanted to show out for Riley.

But in my mind, I played like a bum. I couldn't put the ball in the basket to save my life. I went to the hole with abandon, but nothing dropped. So, I focused instead on rebounding. I was a force on the boards, pulling down sixteen rebounds. I dropped one playmaking dime after another. Took three charges. After the game, Riley approached me. I thought he was going to be disappointed because my offense was so weak.

"That's what I'm talking about, son," he said excitedly. "That fire is what I'm looking for. Play like that every night and there's no limit to how good you can be. That's what the fuck I'm talking about."

Riley taught me the true meaning of the word "disposition." It was one of his favorite words, and he would repeat it over and over. How you carry yourself. Your body language. How you react when things aren't going right. The image you put out for others to see.

For all our promise, the Heat got off to a terrible start, losing our first seven games and eleven of our first fourteen. Riley wasn't happy, but he didn't push the panic button. He was too cool for that. While our record didn't reflect our talent, there was a sense that things would come together soon. Wade was spectacular early on and would make the kind of athletic plays that left you in awe.

One of my close friends on the team was Queens native Rafer Alston, who grew up not far from me and was a certified New York City legend. I was a few years younger than Rafer and had looked up to him when I was a kid. There wasn't anyone from New York who came up after Rafer who didn't emulate him in some way.

Better known as Skip to My Lou, he was in his fifth year—and with his third team—in the NBA after rising to fame at New York's legendary Rucker Park in Harlem. Pat Riley loved his toughness and ability to manage an offense. His role was to back up Dwyane Wade, who started at point. But Skip was just trying to do anything to stay on the team.

He had a nonguaranteed deal and worried daily whether or not he would be let go. If he made it to January 11, the Heat had to lock him in for the rest of the year. The morning of the eleventh, he got the good news that his contract was guaranteed for the remainder of the season.

To celebrate the news, I organized a trip to our favorite strip club. It was great to see him sit back and relax. I just felt like it was one boy from Queens looking out for another. He ended up starting thirteen of the next sixteen games and was a key piece of our playoff run.

About halfway through the season, Liza and the kids moved in, so the shenanigans at the house pretty much came to a standstill. We still occasionally went to strip clubs, but I came home at a decent hour to be respectful to Liza. I still enjoyed all Miami had to offer, but we had gotten the orgies and rendezvous with strippers out of our system for the most part. For a while after Liza moved in, my life began to resemble the kind of existence I'd always dreamed of, and we did family things every weekend.

There were barbecues, birthday parties, and movie nights. We went to restaurants as a family. My kids went to the beach for the first time. Seeing them run down to the water and then flee the surf as it came in is one of the most vivid memories of my life. Destiny was five and learning to ride a bike and developing a love for reading. I'd regularly take her and LJ to the bookstore to buy books, puzzles, and educational games. Our backyard became the center for most of our family activities. I taught LJ to swim, and he took to the water like a dolphin. We had a rule that if you were standing within one foot of the edge of the pool, no matter who you were or what you were wearing, you got pushed in. More than a few cell phones were destroyed that year in Miami.

For the first time in my life, I felt like a real dad. Putting smiles on my kids' faces was rewarding beyond words. Giving them a safe environment where they had everything they could want was priceless. I had something I cared about more than myself. Most importantly, I kept a vow that I had made to myself. I didn't become my father. I did it the right way. That's the most important way my children were different from me. They had a father they could be proud of.

I had stopped smoking almost completely. Riley was pleased with my punctuality and professionalism, and as a result, he pushed me even harder.

"Think Magic Johnson," Riley would say. "Magic Johnson, son!"

"Yes, sir!" I always responded.

I knew how important Magic was to Riley. There was no one he held in higher regard. As a result of clean living and my newfound laser focus, I was playing the best basketball of my career. As a team we hovered around .500 and were fighting to make the playoffs by late spring. I went on a tear.

My confidence was high after recording a near triple double (sixteen points, nine assists, and seven rebounds) on March 4, 2004, against the Milwaukee Bucks. But I needed a game to establish myself as the catalyst of the team and propel us toward the playoffs. Enter the 45–15 Sacramento Kings, two days later. As we walked onto the floor, I could see Pat Riley down the hall at the end of the tunnel leading out to the court. He lowered his head and stared directly at me.

"Carry us!" he said as I ran by. "Carry us, O!"

I did. I carved my way to the basket. I set up my teammates. I ran the break. I was a terror on the boards. Went after every rebound. Kings forward Chris Webber's head nearly spun off his shoulders trying to guard me.

When it was over, I recorded a monster triple double: thirty points, nineteen rebounds, and eleven assists. To this day, it is the only such game in Miami Heat history. I went on to record five more double doubles in the next three weeks, including twenty-six points, eighteen rebounds, and four assists on March 26, against the Mavericks.

I led the Heat to a 9–1 record, putting us squarely back in the playoff mix. I was named Player of the Month in March, the only time in my career I was awarded the honor.

I was in such a good place in my life.

19

After being eliminated 4–2 by the Pacers in the second round of the playoffs, we had our exit meetings and then bid Miami farewell for a month or so.

I'd had one of my best seasons ever, averaging 17.1 points, 9.4 rebounds, and 4.1 assists, and I felt certain I was on the brink of making my first All-Star Game. With First Team All-Rookie superstar Dwyane Wade, Caron Butler, and myself, we had the best young core in the league and looked to be a major factor in the championship chase for years to come.

As is the case when the season ends, everybody headed off in their own directions to get away from basketball. I did what I did at the beginning of every off-season and flew back to New York. Back in those days you had to turn your phone off during air travel. When we landed, I turned on my phone and it sounded like a pinball machine. It was beeping and buzzing and blinking like crazy. For a split second a lightning bolt of fear passed through me. With so many messages, something big must have happened.

The majority of the calls were from my agent, Jeff Schwartz. Why in the world was Jeff calling me, I wondered. We were locked in for another three years. Something was brewing. Something big. Like 320 pounds big.

"Miami is trying to move you," said Jeff, once I got him on the phone.

"What?! We just got there," I said. "I just killed the entire year."

"Well, they're trying to trade you for Shaq."

Shaquille O'Neal, the most coveted center in the NBA . . . told you it was big. I was stunned and hurt. Pat Riley had told me he absolutely loved what I brought to the table and that I was in the Heat's long-term plans. But damn . . . they wanted Shaq. I knew that Riley had wanted Shaq for years. Every coach and GM did. He was the piece to everyone's championship dreams, so I couldn't be that upset. I'd trade me for Shaq, too.

The proposed trade had the Heat sending me, Caron Butler, Brian Grant, and a first-round draft pick to the Lakers in exchange for Shaquille O'Neal.

Riley had been working on it for weeks unbeknownst to me. While we were in the air, the media had falsely reported that the trade was complete. This was why Jeff was calling me. I had a trade kicker in my contract, which meant that if I got traded within my first year in Miami, I received a 15 percent bonus.

I took in Jeff's words through a haze of disbelief, and he kept having to repeat himself until it sank in. My mind raced as I played out the season in my head, wondering if there was anything I could have done differently. Mainly I thought about my budding relationship with Riley, one of my all-time basketball heroes. I thought he loved me. I felt unwanted. Worse, I felt betrayed.

This is why players are constantly repeating the mantra "It's a business." Because it's 100 percent true. There's no loyalty. If you convince yourself otherwise, you'll end up getting hurt . . . like I just had.

To get my mind off the impending trade and my feelings of rejection, I went to the New York Sports Club to work out. I got up some shots, worked on my ball handling, and did some light weight work. I burned off some of my aggression, but every person I ran into at the club had questions about the trade. The actor Taye Diggs quizzed me about the deal in between sets.

After the workout, Greg and I sat in the cafeteria, still stunned at what was unfolding. *Live! With Regis and Kelly* host Regis Philbin startled me with a rather excited intro.

"Hey, Lamar! What's the situation with the trade? It's crazy!" he said in that familiar staccato delivery. "Congratulations!"

I was having a hard time taking it all in. I was trying not to mope, but I loved Miami and didn't want to leave. Plus, the prospect of having Shaq, D-Wade, and myself would give us one of the most unique lineups in NBA history and make us the odds-on favorite to win the championship and start our own dynasty.

I got back to my room at the Phillips Club hotel and the phone started heating up again. Jeff told me that it was within his power to take me out of the deal and replace me with Eddie Jones. Riley was definitely into the idea and wanted to keep me in Miami if it was at all possible. But the Lakers wouldn't do the deal without me. Lakers general manager Mitch Kupchak wouldn't budge. He had visions of a dynamic duo of me and Kobe Bryant. Riley thought he could pull off the trade without me, but his hands were tied. The Lakers weren't going to ship

Shaq off without getting what they wanted in return. I was the key to the trade.

There was a bright side. I'd get a $7.4 million bonus to go back to Los Angeles, and I'd be playing for the most storied franchise in NBA history alongside the game's best player in Kobe Bryant. That's not bad.

My phone rang. It was Riley.

"Hey, I'm sorry we're at this point," said Riley.

"I don't know what to say," I said meekly. "I know you have to do—"

He cut me off.

"I just want you to know I love you," Riley said. I could hear that it was difficult for him to get the words out. His voice cracked and he began to choke up. So did I. There was a knot in my throat, and I hoped he'd keep speaking so I wouldn't have to. His words confirmed what I had hoped to be true—that Pat Riley loved me. He cared about me as more than just a basketball player. In that moment, that meant more to me than bonuses and trade clauses. It was the most difficult talk I've ever had with a basketball executive.

There was a long pause. I could hear him sighing on the other end. The guilt as he exhaled was palpable. He hinted that nothing was set in stone.

"O, this thing came out of nowhere," Riley said. "These things move so damn fast sometimes. But . . ."

When he called me O, I knew he was sincere, as his voice was always full of honesty when he did that.

Still, I didn't say anything. Another pause. This one longer and more excruciating than the first. Just air on the phone. But I wouldn't break the silence.

"I'll pull it," said Riley, completely shocking me. "I'll pull it, O. But I need to call you back."

Greg and I freaked out. Every kind of emotion possible was pouring out of me, yet I didn't know how to react. I desperately waited for the phone to ring to get more information. Five minutes later my phone rang. It was Jeff.

Riley had called Heat owner Micky Arison after he got off the phone with me. Arison rejected any deal in which O'Neal didn't become the newest member of the Miami Heat. The deal would go on as scheduled. My heart dropped.

"Also," Jeff explained, "Pat Riley is forbidden to have any further contact with you. Their lawyers just called me. Riley will not be calling you back. It's over."

I hung up the phone and put my head in my hands. I felt like crying.

20

Before the trade to the Lakers, I received one of the biggest honors in my career as I was named to the 2004 US Men's Olympic basketball team. As a kid I was transfixed by the original Dream Team and had always fantasized about being an Olympian and representing the United States.

I would join a team that included veterans Tim Duncan, Allen Iverson, and Amar'e Stoudemire. It would also be an international coming-out party for LeBron James, Carmelo Anthony, and my Heat teammate Dwyane Wade, who were coming off brilliant rookie seasons.

But the joy of being named to the twelve-man roster quickly turned to anxiety when Olympic officials informed me that I would have to pass a drug test before officially joining the team. It hadn't even occurred to me. Obviously, doping was a big thing, but performance-enhancing drugs are basically a nonissue in the NBA. That stuff's for track-and-field and cyclists. Didn't matter. Everyone has to be tested and it's serious business.

We all had relocated back to LA when I got the call from USA Basketball that a drug tester would be coming to my house in a few days to administer the screening. There was absolutely no way I was going to pass. I'd been smoking weed every day that summer. Panic set in. *What if I fail?* That would be my third failed drug test in four years. Would people's patience finally run out? Would it even count as a strike against me as far as the NBA was concerned?

We weren't going to find out. We started googling "fake penises" and studied different ways to beat a drug test. After an exhaustive search we ordered a giant rubber black cock to arrive the next day. When I filled the sample cup and handed it back to the tester, the urine had to be warm to prove it just came out of my body. People tried to evade detection by having a cup of clean urine waiting in a cupboard in their bathroom, but that didn't work with the USOC. That pee had better be body temperature.

Robert Montgomery of NBA security, who administered the test, pulled into the driveway and knocked on the door. That was the signal for my trainer, Robbie Davis, to urinate into the reservoir of the phallus, which was hidden in the balls. He'd never done drugs a day in his life, so his piss was guaranteed clean. He handed me the rubber penis and left the bathroom as I strapped it on.

Montgomery entered the bathroom and handed me the cup. He was standing about two feet behind me as I turned around toward the toilet. The reality of what I was doing started to set in and I got a little nervous. This was absolutely crazy, but crazy was my only option at the time. I unzipped my pants and carefully slid the fake penis through the zipper hole. To get the pee to come out of the tip, I had to squeeze the shaft repeatedly.

I had to be careful to disguise my motions because it's an unnatural way to relieve oneself. Even though we put this thing through several trial runs, I was paranoid it wouldn't work.

Plus, the dude was standing right behind me. I was extremely careful not to drop the sample cup after I filled it, because with the tester at my house, it's not like we could come up with another fresh batch.

I filled the cup and then finished off in the toilet to give the perception that I was actually using the bathroom. Then I handed Montgomery a hot cup of piss. He stuck a thermometer in the cup to gauge the temperature. Montgomery, satisfied that the pee was mine, said, "Welcome to Team USA." Just like that he was gone. When he pulled out of the driveway, we all breathed a sigh of relief. That was a serious risk. I was cool under fire, but my nerves were rattled.

I went out back to smoke.

Several days later we were off to Jacksonville to begin eighteen days of training that would lead up to the games in Athens, Greece. From there it was off to Germany, Serbia, and Montenegro, and finally Istanbul. Despite the mix of veterans and rookies, most who had never played together before, the team's personalities jelled fairly quickly. Perhaps more than any other Olympic team in recent memory, this squad liked to party. Much to the chagrin of NBA security, we craved the night and whatever adventure came with it.

Our security detail was like no other in USA Basketball history. This was the first post-9/11 Olympic games, and both the NBA and the USOC weren't taking any chances. In Turkey we were in the most extravagant five-star hotel, and a bomb exploded less than a mile away. Security immediately rounded up players and coaches and took us to a bunker below, where we had to wait until there was no threat.

It was out of the question for us to leave the hotel without security. They had to know where we were at all times. Not even players' friends or family could leave the hotel unattended. It was a drag to say the least, and sometimes it wasn't worth the hassle to go out, so we spent a lot of time in our rooms. Guys were starting to get tired of that before we even got to Greece.

One day, Allen Iverson and Stephon Marbury came up with a plan to shake security and organized a players-only night out. Iverson was our leader and the oldest player on the team. We all looked up to him, and when he spoke, we listened. He was a hero to many of us. Guys were in awe of him, and we tried to soak up every minute with Iverson. He was our OG.

Nearly the whole team organized in the lobby for our secret night out. LeBron, Carmelo, and A.I. had on 3XL white T-shirts, so we kind of stood out. It wasn't exactly the most clandestine operation, but somehow eleven professional basketball players—everyone except for Tim Duncan—managed to duck out a side door and jump in a line of cabs. Back then, Utah forward and Turkey native Mehmet Okur owned one of the dopest nightclubs in Turkey. It had a glitzy outdoor area and a massive interior with five floors, which was accessible by boat.

There were insane two-hundred-foot yachts parked on the docks out back. Iverson was leading the charge as we headed inside. I'd never seen so many beautiful women in one spot at the same time. There were women of nearly every ethnicity with every skin tone and hair texture imaginable. Liquor was flowing. Music was pulsating. Guys were hooking up all over the place. It felt like a scene out of a movie.

About three in the morning, Iverson had seen enough and wanted to organize the transportation so we didn't have to wait and risk getting mobbed. The moment we stepped outside, though, we were swarmed by a dozen paparazzi. Flashbulbs were going off like crazy. Somebody tipped off our handlers to the fact that we were there, and in an instant, three giant NBA security vans pulled up and came to a screeching halt outside the club. Security personnel jumped out and they were not pleased.

The jig was up.

We arrived in Greece on August 13, 2004, the day after our epic night out, and there would be no more evading security. We were under many watchful eyes from the moment we arrived until the moment we left. After much deliberation it was decided that the team would stay on the $800 million RMS *Queen Mary 2*, a gigantic, luxurious ocean liner that was docked in a special Olympic zone, which was protected by commandos, motion detectors, gunboats, helicopters, and sensors that could detect swimmers in the water under the boat. It was a brand-new boat and the longest passenger ship ever built, stretching 1,132 feet . . . nearly a quarter of a mile.

The decision to stay on the *Queen Mary* and not in Olympic Village with the other athletes ruffled some feathers and was derided in the press. But the NBA considered the security risk to be too great. It was an enormous security undertaking just to get the team on and off the boat every day. You had to go through several different security checks whether you were boarding or leaving the boat. We had fun the couple times we visited the Olympic Village, but we mostly stayed on the boat. Once we managed to hit a strip club in Greece that was packed with beautiful Russian women, but that was it.

The ship had dozens of restaurants, a cinema, a shopping mall, a theater for plays, a library, a wine bar, countless works of art, and even a planetarium. But apart from some British dignitaries and Saudi princes, we were the only ones on the ship, so it felt like a ghost town.

We spent most of our time at the ship's club called G32, named after the ocean liner's hull number, on the second deck, where there was a huge dance floor and several bars where we'd go drink every night.

One night, A.I. stumbled into a cigar room and proceeded to organize meet-ups at 8 PM every night, where a bunch of guys would go to smoke cigars and trade stories. Iverson dubbed the group the Cigar Club. He held court and told wild stories about his life and career. Nobody wanted to miss them because you never knew what you were going to hear.

The Cigar Club was an education on the lives of the world's best basketball players. No subject was off-limits. Near the end of the almost three-week run of the Cigar Club, Chuck (only A.I.'s close friends and family got to call him "Bubba-chuck," or "Chuck" for short) told one of his best stories. Several years prior, during the epic Jay-Z versus Nas hip-hop beef,

Nas dropped his infamous diss track "Ether." Jay-Z quickly responded with a track of his own called "Supa Ugly."

In the first lines of the third verse, Jay referenced how both he and Iverson had flings with Carmen Bryan, Nas's girlfriend and the mother of one of his children. In the lyrics Jay raps: "Me and the boy A.I. got more in common / Than just ballin' and rhymin' / Get it? / More in Carmen."

Iverson said the day the song, came out he was driving with his wife. "I'm listening to the song, thinking this joint is hot," said Iverson. "I mess around and turn it up. Then that line comes and I'm like what?! My wife looks dead at me and slaps me across the face! Slaps the shit out of me."

Everyone was in tears. Cracking up. But nobody wanted to interrupt. Everybody wanted him to keep going. Chuck just puffed his cigar. "So I'm pissed, right. Just pissed. So, you know what I did?" asked Iverson. "I called Jay-Z up. I said why the fuck you put my name in that song? Why you drag me into your bullshit?"

There was a pause on the phone.

"Yo, it was just wordplay," said Jay-Z. "I didn't mean it like that. It's no big deal."

"But I'm married with kids, man," replied A.I. "You can't put me out there like that."

"Yo, don't take it that serious," Jay-Z said calmly. "Mike Jordan is back."

Then Jay-Z hung up the phone.

Everyone just started clapping at the story. The young guns like LeBron and Melo were in awe, soaking up every moment. When LeBron was a kid, his idol wasn't Jordan; it was Allen

Iverson. He wanted to be like Chuck from the headband to the shooting sleeve to the impact he had on the game. You could see how valuable these nightly get-togethers were for him. And me, too. Being with the guys on that trip was one of the best experiences of my life.

However, it was another story entirely on the court, as that 2004 team was one of the most disappointing US Olympic basketball teams ever. We were disjointed and never really clicked. It's the only team since 1992, when the US started sending pros, that failed to win the gold medal. The three losses we suffered were the most ever in Olympic competition, and the nineteen-point drubbing at the hands of Puerto Rico was the biggest loss by Team USA ever.

From the start, no one got along with coach Larry Brown's style or substitution patterns. He was an old-school disciplinarian who took the fun out of the experience for a lot of guys. Playing basketball in the summer is supposed to be fun. Brown overlooked more talented upstarts like LeBron and Melo in favor of veterans like Shawn Marion and Richard Jefferson. LeBron, Melo, and D-Wade were so upset, they gathered in the ship's computer room at midnight one night and feverishly looked up next season's NBA schedule to see when they would be playing against Marion and Jefferson.

We came home with a bronze medal that no one even wanted. It was hard not to be upset with the result, and it lingered with many of us. One positive was that I played really well and ended up being one of our most consistent players. I averaged 9.3 points and 5.8 rebounds on 57 percent shooting while starting all eight games. Even though it wasn't gold, I was still happy to get my medal. In many ways it represented how far I'd come. When I got home, I gave it to my son, LJ, and he put it on his dresser, where it remains to this day.

21

've had sex with more than two thousand women.

I don't remember most of their names. Many of them were one-night stands. There were too many strippers to count. It wasn't a big deal, but often I would pay them. I would just give them money in the morning. I never thought less of them. I would make love to them and leave $2,000 on the dresser. It was understood that they would be gone when I got out of the shower because I usually had to be at practice or shootaround.

I have been obsessed with sex as long as I can remember. I love to touch women, and I need to feel close to women and feel their skin on mine. To touch a woman is to feel safe. The physical contact is something that I need. It doesn't even have to always be sex. If it's spooning on the bed, it will satisfy me just the same. I just need the connection.

And I know you won't believe this, but I don't remember my first time. That sounds crazy, right? I think I was fourteen. It was during the two-year period right after my mother died, and I've purged almost every memory of that time. My first memory of sex is with Liza when I was in the eleventh grade. It was the summer of 1996 after I came back from Las Vegas. We conceived Destiny, our first child, the following year.

I've been looking for my mother ever since she died. I looked for her in the women I took home. I used sex to fill the void . . .

to make me feel complete. I wanted to be loved, but I could never find love. I could be physically fulfilled, but I was always left emotionally empty. I would fuck five or six girls a week, but my demons tormented me the one night I went home alone. I needed women as an outlet . . . an escape. But this does not come without problems. Most of my sex had been unprotected, and I've paid for plenty of abortions over the years. I'm not proud of it. It's the law and legal, but I don't feel proud about it at all.

I am a sex addict.

My sex addiction and my cocaine addiction go hand in hand. They afflicted me from the moment I woke up until I laid my head down to sleep. Try this with a day job.

The first time I did cocaine, sometime in the summer of 2004, was an eye-opening experience. I was at the Shore Club, a high-end hotel in Miami that caters to celebrities and the super-rich. I was at the pool with a bunch of friends and happened to walk past a rich white couple sitting poolside. The man got up from a lounge chair and asked me if I had any cocaine. It was a weird question to which I gave a really strange response.

"I think I can get some," I replied. I don't know why I said that.

I walked over to my boys and they slipped me a little baggie of coke.

I was a little nervous to do it. I didn't know how it was going to make me feel. Worse, I was afraid that I would like it.

And my fears were confirmed. The first time I did cocaine it felt like I had a full-body orgasm. Actually, I kind of did.

The stranger, his wife, and I went into a secluded area away from the pool. The woman was about thirty-five, blonde, and beautiful. She looked like a Playboy Playmate straight out of the 1970s. They were both excited that I could score so quickly. They were also excited to meet a famous black basketball player. We sat at a little table and the woman told her husband to leave. He did so dutifully and quickly.

"About fucking time," she said.

We emptied the bag onto the table and I pulled my American Express Black Card out of my pocket and began separating the coke into several lines. I didn't know exactly what I was doing, but I had seen it done in movies. The woman took off her top. She had amazing tan lines. I stared at her tits as she leaned over and snorted a line with a rolled-up one-hundred-dollar bill.

She handed the bill to me. Fuck it. I leaned over, put the bill to my nose, and inhaled with my left nostril. My mind went blank. I immediately jumped up. The rush was like nothing I had ever felt before or since. It went straight to my cock, and I got hard instantly. She did the third line, and I did the fourth. The woman then got down on her knees, pulled my shorts down, and took my manhood in her mouth.

I couldn't believe how it felt, and I came after a couple minutes. She got up, pulled her top back on, and fluffed her hair.

"It was nice to meet you," she said before walking away.

I stood there wondering what the fuck just happened. I was blown away. A new dimension had come into my life. Cocaine. And the way it made me feel. How it went straight to my cock.

I had to feel that way again. Like, right then. I wanted to fuck on cocaine.

I spent the better part of the next fifteen years chasing the feeling of that first high. I needed to feel like that again. I would kill myself to do it if I had to.

Cocaine is a hell of a drug.

Once we got back to Los Angeles at the end of summer 2004, I decided to make a few changes for what would be my second fresh start in as many years. I moved to a new place right on the ocean.

It felt good to be back in LA with its familiar routes, beautiful views, and old haunts. Al Harris and Kamal McQueen were still living out in the Valley, and I was looking forward to reconnecting with them. As usual, Greg moved in with me and began to take care of all house-related issues and remained my driver/manager.

In late September, the Lakers players began to return to LA and gather for pickup games at the practice facility in El Segundo, just south of LAX. I was coming off my best season as a pro and was in great shape to start the season thanks to playing for Team USA in Greece.

But there was one person in camp who was already in better shape than anyone. In fact, in his first eight years in the league, I don't think he was ever out of shape. I marveled at the way he treated his body. At twenty-six, with three NBA championships and six All-Star appearances, Kobe Bryant was on a meteoric rise and had without a doubt claimed the title of best player in the NBA.

Everything Kobe did was in the pursuit of perfection. Whether it was how he conditioned his mind and body, religiously watched film, or competed like a demon on the floor, it was easy to be in awe of him. When you were around Kobe, he either rubbed off on you or grated on you. He set the tone and it was up to everyone else to adjust.

But this was a different Kobe Bryant and a different Lakers team. Phil Jackson had retired and taken his three rings and four Finals appearances in the last four years with him. Shaq passed me in the night on the way to Miami. For the first time in decades, the Lakers were a rebuilding team.

The previous year, Kobe had played under a dark cloud in the form of a year-long sexual assault investigation stemming from an incident in a hotel room in Eagle, Colorado, in which a hotel employee accused him of rape. The hearings and discoveries dominated the headlines, and Kobe had the poorest season of his prime years.

Shortly after I got back to LA, the charges against Kobe were dropped because his accuser refused to testify. Although Kobe's public image took a beating, and his reputation as the clean-cut face of the league had been shattered, Kobe was determined to put everything behind him and focus all his energy into basketball.

You could sense that Kobe wasn't the happiest person in the world. He had narrowly avoided what would have been a psychologically draining and image-crushing trial—win or lose—that would have changed the course of his life. The mental anguish of losing basketball and facing a decade-long prison sentence took its toll on Kobe.

Still, he arrived at training camp in phenomenal shape. From pickup games to shooting drills, he was ultra-competitive and would be furious if he lost. Or worse, if someone's lack-luster play contributed to that loss. And Kobe talked a lot. He threw elbows while berating opponents and teammates alike. When he walked into the gym, the tenor of the room changed noticeably. It was all business. If pickup games started at eleven in the morning, Kobe would likely have already been up since five. Sometimes I'd just be getting home at that point.

I never had another teammate with the drive Kobe had. Even when his personal life was in utter turmoil he never lost that drive. But I knew being in such close proximity to someone as competitive as Kobe would be perfect for me. In those early days of pickup ball and practice, Kobe put everyone through what he called his "vetting process" to see what they were made of.

Kobe would walk right up to you and ask, "What are you gonna do?"

"I ain't scared of you," I would shoot back. I had to let him know right away.

He dished out loads of trash talk to see how we'd respond. He was hard-fucking-core. You were no one to him unless you proved yourself first. If you got rattled and didn't hand it right back, you would immediately lose points in his book. And he would come harder at you with the intention of running you off. If he couldn't trust you in practice, he wouldn't trust you during the games. But I'm from Queens, so nothing he could say to me was new.

As storied as the franchise was, the mystique didn't feel quite as I expected it. The Lakers were still the jewel in the NBA's crown, but the 2004–2005 Lakers weren't Riley's Lakers. Or Phil Jackson's, either. Over the summer the Lakers hired Rudy Tomjanovich to a five-year, $30 million contract to guide the team back to glory. But as intense as Rudy was on the bench and in his preparation, he ran a pretty loose ship with his players. The team had a decidedly different feel than the way Riley presided over the Heat, which I had grown to love.

My friends and trainer could now fly on the team plane and show up to practice whenever they wanted. Riley didn't even let my boys attend team dinners at Joe's Stone Crab.

The team was uneven and disjointed, but as predicted, Kobe helped me elevate my play, and I averaged 15.2 points, 10.2 rebounds, 3.7 assists, and a career-high 47 percent shooting from the field. But we were a lost cause, finishing 34–48 and missing the playoffs for the first time in eleven years. The eleventh-place finish in the Western Conference standings was the worst in franchise history.

I was glad to be back in Los Angeles, but as a whole, we were ready to put this forgettable season behind us.

My love affair with cocaine wasn't going to go away. You know how you meet a new girl and fall head over heels in love and can't see enough of that person? Yeah, that's what happened when I first did coke. And when you first do it, you don't realize the power it has. Both the potency and the control it has over you. I started to surround myself with people who did the same thing. It's not hard to find enablers. They are a dime a dozen. They want to bask in your fame, and they'll provide you with a fix. Sign me up, I thought.

The Shore Club in Miami became our home away from home, leaving work in LA for escape on the other side of the country. It was a playground where nothing was off-limits and rules didn't exist. When the night was either too debaucherous, scandalous, or illegal, I knew the comfortable confines of my favorite beach paradise would be someplace to go where the only thing that would fade away faster than my inhibitions was my better judgment.

On some nights it seemed like there was almost as much cocaine in South Beach as there was sand. As my drug use slowly escalated, I found that strippers made cocaine better and coke made sex better. I felt the kind of invincibility that basketball, money, and fame never brought me. That was a high in itself.

As my cocaine use transformed from experimental to habitual, I hid it from my closest friends—my New York crew. Greg, Al, and Kamal would have flipped if they found out the level I had taken it to. As far as they were concerned, this was a pastime for the new group of friends that I so easily let into my trusted circle.

My collection of friends grew as fast as my "hobby," and sometime early during my stint with the Lakers, I met music producer Scott Storch. He was at the top of his game producing music in his Miami studio for the likes of 50 Cent, Beyoncé, Snoop Dogg, and even Paris Hilton. At his height in the mid-2000s, he was one of the biggest hip-hop producers in the game. He'd charge $250,000 for a single beat.

Scott lived in a $10 million mansion in Palm Island, Florida, and had a fleet of twenty cars. It was like he lived in a music video. But Scott had a way of winning people over by telling them what they wanted to hear. His atmosphere was a twenty-four-hour party, swirling, pulsating, and scooping up everyone in its path with gale-force velocity.

But it was also cool that Scott was a self-made man from Long Island who accomplished what no one thought he could, and he always tried to hold on to that New York grittiness. He had everything . . . including cocaine. I'd spend hours . . . days . . . at his mansion with pounds of coke everywhere. It was modern-day Tony Montana shit.

"Okay, I'm reloaded!"

I used to love that quote from *Scarface*. Because I always reloaded.

When you have a burgeoning drug habit, surrounding yourself with enablers and habitual users is one thing, but rolling with people who have bigger narcotic appetites than yours is like hitting fast-forward on your drug problem.

Coke was everywhere. If I wasn't crushing it at Scott's mansion or at the Shore Club with famous one-name superstars, I would sneak it back to my house in California. It was easier if Liza and the kids weren't visiting. (Liza had moved back to New York after Miami.) Definitely if Greg and Kamal weren't in LA. I was still perfecting my standard speech about how it wasn't mine. *It's for the strippers. I give them coke and they fuck. I just want to make sure they have a good time.*

I was a drug addict plain and simple. I had arrived at this terrible, unwanted, inevitable conclusion almost on cruise control. It felt like destiny. I had been building the résumé before I had ever rolled my first joint. Or, to be clearer, others had been writing it for me.

My father physically abused my mother, my only source of protection, right in front of me. She screamed and cried and struggled. I was helpless and felt like a coward because I couldn't do a damn thing about it. It stripped me of any power before I knew what those things meant. I'd see my mom beaten. Then we'd go to sleep several feet from one another in our twin beds in the upstairs bedroom of my grandmother's house on 131st. I could hear Mom struggling to turn over. Her sighs clouded the air like a suffocating black smoke that would be way more destructive than any puff of narcotic smoke I could ever inhale.

These were things that I would never recover from. I haven't to this day.

My strung-out father disappeared. People made fun of me when they saw him bingeing. I was an only child and any positive view of myself was taken from me before I could even comprehend that I had it in the first place.

I convinced myself that everything I was doing was destiny, but I cringed when I heard Cathy Odom's voice in those moments of indecision and despair. "Lamar, you are your own light," she'd tell me. "You are a light for all others."

But at Scott Storch's house or the Shore Club, that light went out. I was still, unbeknownst to myself, two years away from the pit of hell, but at least I could get high right now. On one particular weekend at Scott's house, I poured out what I thought was a reasonable portion and used my Black Card to divide the lines. I would snort each nostril. The lines looked like they went on forever. I would wait for the drip. Then the aftertaste.

But most of all I craved the rush, the high. That's why you do coke. It's the best friend you've ever had. All the blood rushed to my cock. I wanted to fuck. I'd get two strippers from the club. Always two. Money on the dresser and gone by the time I got out of the shower. I did this almost every night.

I chased the high, hit after hit, wanting it to feel like that first time. If it didn't work, I'd do another line. Then another.

One night, after several hours of chasing that first time, I had no clue what time it was or even how in the world I'd ended up at Scott's mansion. A strange feeling began to come over my body. Time slowed down. I couldn't swallow. My body was burning. I was cold. Then I was hot. I had what I thought was the worst case of nausea ever. A wave of anxiety like I'd never felt in my life hit me like a tidal wave. The fear paralyzed me.

I tried to stand, but my 230-pound body felt like air. I lifted off the ground . . . floating to nowhere and everywhere. The light went out and I crashed to the floor. I couldn't breathe. My eyes rolled back in my head. My lungs tightened. My heart fluttered.

People rushed into the room screaming, but I couldn't hear anything. Someone threw a towel over my head and ushered me through the back door of University of Miami Hospital. The official diagnosis was that I was dehydrated and needed IVs and fluids to bring me back around. Yeah, that was it. Anything but the truth.

But I knew the truth.

That was the first time I overdosed. I came within minutes of dying. I nearly killed myself chasing that high.

Depression is like having a demon with a sword at the back of your neck every step you take, but when you turn, he won't talk to you. The fact that you can't look him in the eye, or are unable to, is the most frightening of all. You don't want to acknowledge him. But he's there. His presence compounded my anxiety. Where do I go? How do I escape? How do I sleep? Everything affects everything else, and no escape is ever good enough . . . not even the cocaine and strippers. You know ahead of time nothing will ever make the demon go away. He will always be there. Drugs are your best defense and worst enemy.

I was no longer in control.

That demon will always be on the back of a twelve-year-old kid. That's when I first saw him. A kid with no power. It's easy to torment a kid who can't fight back. But I'm not twelve anymore, and that's the most frustrating thing about it. I'm thirty-nine as I write this. I'm not supposed to be afraid or weak.

But I am.

My mother is still dead. Sometimes I had to ask myself if I was, too.

After my overdose, doctors begged me to slow down, get rest, and eat right. *Take care of your body, Lamar; it's the only one you've got.* Back at home, I felt like I'd been hit by a train. I stayed in bed for days and was frustrated at how weak my body felt. I was angry at myself for letting it come to this. I vowed I'd straighten out and get my life back on track. But deep down I could feel it coming, festering, waiting, calling my name. The demon was gone, but I knew he'd be back. But no! This time I would win. I had to.

Training camp for the 2005–06 season was only five weeks away.

22

When Rudy Tomjanovich stepped down as the Lakers' head coach in the middle of the 2004–2005 season, the organization was prepared to go on an exhaustive coaching search to find the ideal candidate. But that never materialized because Kobe Bryant only had one coach in mind: Phil Jackson. Kobe worked extremely well with Jackson and wanted someone he trusted. So, on June 15, 2005, the Lakers hired Phil Jackson after just one season away from the team.

When Phil returned to El Segundo, he brought his intricate yet highly successful triangle offense, which was masterminded by his longtime assistant Tex Winter. The Bulls had won six championships with its triple-post offense, and the Lakers won three more in the span of twelve years, so everyone knew it worked. It was based on both player and ball movement that was designed to encourage team play while not detracting from individual talent—all in the interest of getting the best possible shot.

To be honest, the triangle offense confused me at first, and it took me a while to pick it up. I would sometimes be out of place, make the wrong pass, or force a shot when it wasn't necessary. I could see Kobe getting frustrated with me, and he'd do his own coaching. There was something that just resonated more clearly when someone like Kobe, who could run any offense, pointed out things on the floor to help the learning process.

"We're going to use you in a lot of areas," Kobe explained to me one day in practice. "The elbow, mid-post, short corner to break apart defenses. I'm going to see a lot of overload defenses, so with you flashing to the high post, you've got the talent to be able to catch the ball and look opposite to make those reads and make the right pass. When I get doubled and make that pass, most teams don't have anybody with your length and size to make the right pass. We'll win championships with that hockey-assist play because when I kick it to you, you'll be the one making decisions."

Kobe trusted me.

That was really the cornerstone of how well we worked together. He understood the value of what I brought to the table and how to bring it out of me. Honestly, it took a couple seasons to get the kind of patience and understanding of spacing to make it work for us, but obviously the end results were worth it.

In Phil's first year back, we ended up making the 2005–2006 playoffs despite dealing with injuries to Kobe and me. We even went up 3–1 against the second seed, the Phoenix Suns, in the first round. Ultimately, however, their depth, pace, and the floor generalship of eventual MVP Steve Nash was too much to overcome, and we lost in seven games. But we were headed in the right direction.

In the fall of 2005, Liza was pregnant with our third child, and the baby was due on Christmas Day. We made all of the necessary arrangements for a family that's expecting. Liza and the kids moved back to Los Angeles so we could be together for the birth.

I bought a Range Rover, which I got off Jason Kidd for cheap—like $9,000—so Liza could have more freedom getting around with the children.

I was so excited for the baby's arrival, but the only problem was that the Lakers would be playing in Miami on Christmas, and I would miss the birth. But during a home stand in mid-December, Liza began having contractions and was rushed to UCLA Medical Center in Santa Monica, the same hospital where LJ was born nearly four years earlier.

I was convinced we were going to have a second girl. I just thought that's what the universe was going to give us. Since we didn't know the sex before the baby was born, we hadn't picked out a name. It didn't help that Liza and I couldn't come close to agreeing.

For boy names, my first choice was Luke, after my close teammate Luke Walton. I was going for basketball names. I thought Dominique would be great, too. But Liza wasn't feeling it. She wanted the name Jayden. Ever since Will Smith and Jada Pinkett Smith named their son Jaden, Liza couldn't get it out of her mind. Plus, it would work for a boy or a girl.

On December 15, we welcomed Jayden Joseph Odom into this world. I held him in my arms and stared directly into his huge brown eyes. The next night the Lakers had a game against the Wizards. As I chipped in fourteen points and eleven rebounds, my feet didn't touch the ground. I thought of my beautiful boy the entire time.

After Jayden was born, Liza wanted to have her tubes tied. She was twenty-four with three children, and we decided that our family was complete. However, when she met with her doctor, he told her about a patient in a similar situation whose infant died at three months from a heart defect. The patient regretted tying her tubes. The doctor stressed that Liza shouldn't do it. And she didn't.

For much of the early part of 2006, life felt right and we were as close a family as we'd ever been. Because Liza was a young mother, she had hired a nanny to help her out with the children. Liza put the kids in a private school in Marina Del Rey, driving them back and forth every day. Destiny went to classes with the son of Brooklyn rapper Notorious B.I.G. His widow, Faith Evans, would drop off and pick up Biggie's son every day. When Destiny got her yearbook, we all gathered around to see the legendary Christopher Wallace's son. He looked like a light-skinned Biggie.

In June 2006, my aunt Sandy passed away. She was the third of Grandma Mildred's daughters. Liza, the kids, and I returned to New York in the middle of the year to pay our respects.

We had bought a home the previous summer in the hidden waterfront town of Atlantic Beach between Queens and Long Island. The plan was for Liza to raise the kids there in the off-season.

She would say that I always got lost in the summer. I would disappear and go my separate way to either Miami or some far corner of New York. We would bicker about it constantly. She thought I was hanging out with my friends in the city too often. And I was. Sure, I would always check in with her when I was out, but because I wasn't present, it was a problem. She wanted me home. I wanted to be in the city.

After the funeral, we stayed at the Atlantic Beach house for the summer. Liza's mother moved in to help take care of our three young children. Liza set up Jayden's room right next to our master bedroom, which was complete with a baby monitor so she could keep tabs on him.

On the morning of June 29, Liza woke up and checked on Jayden as she had done every day since he had been born. She got his bottle ready and walked into his room. He was still, and his blankets were undisturbed from the night before. Liza felt happy. She noticed that he was on his stomach, which was a bit unusual. But he was still sleeping and looked content so she didn't disturb him.

She went downstairs and joined her mother in the kitchen. There was a pot of coffee on the counter. The smell of decaf wafted on the air. The sunlight shone through the bay window, filling the kitchen with natural light.

"Good morning," Liza said cheerily.

"How's Jayden?" her mom asked. "Is he okay?"

Liza stopped in her tracks. Her blood went cold. *Why wouldn't he be okay?*

She dropped her coffee mug and raced back upstairs, taking two steps at a time. She burst into Jayden's room. He was lying there in the exact same position. His blankets were undisturbed, wrapped around him. She picked him up and turned him over.

His face was a dark blue. He wasn't breathing.

Liza screamed hysterically. Liza's mother, a registered nurse, immediately took Jayden.

"Call 911!" Liza's mother screamed. Liza frantically dialed the number.

The operator who answered the phone was distant and emotionless. Liza would recall for years how cold he was. But an ambulance and fire trucks were dispatched in minutes. Emergency crews rushed into the house and dashed upstairs, immediately taking Jayden away in the ambulance. Liza and her mother were screaming uncontrollably. They were still in their pajamas.

"We can't wait for you," said an EMT as the ambulance sped off. A police officer told them to get in his cruiser, and he drove them to the hospital.

I had spent the night partying in Manhattan, and Liza called me from the back of the cruiser.

"Something happened to Jayden," she shouted into the phone.

"What?" I said, waking up in a haze. "What happened to LJ?"

"No! Jayden!"

"I don't understand. What's wrong with LJ?"

For some reason, it just didn't register with me that the problem was with my newborn son. I couldn't comprehend what was happening. I got dressed and took the long journey to South Nassau Communities Hospital, where our entire family was gathering. Liza and her mother called aunts, brothers, sisters, and cousins.

My cousin Sherrod drove me, and it seemed like there was traffic and construction everywhere we turned. I took forever to get to the hospital, and all I could think was that when Liza needed me the most, I wasn't there.

I was the last to arrive at the hospital. I was quickly ushered into a private room where Liza was waiting. The room was freezing, and Liza was wrapped in a hospital blanket. All we knew was that the hospital was running tests. That was the only information they gave us. Fifteen minutes after I got there, a doctor entered the room and grasped Liza's hand. There were tears in the doctor's eyes.

"I'm sorry," she said. "As a mother I've experienced crib death, too."

Crib death.

That was the first time I had ever heard that term. I didn't know what it was. Jayden had died from sudden infant death syndrome. SIDS is when a healthy baby less than a year old dies from unknown causes, usually in his or her crib. Doctors think that babies sleeping on their backs are less likely to die from SIDS. Liza put him to sleep on his back. When she found him in the morning, he was on his stomach.

It just didn't make sense to us. How could our baby just die in his crib? This couldn't be a real thing. I was stunned, numb, almost emotionless. I couldn't move.

I did not cry then. Or the next day. I did not cry for Jayden for three years. I thought if I cried it would make it real. I did not cry so that he might live.

The doctor brought Jayden into the room where Liza and I could hold him one last time. She handed him to Liza. She gripped him tightly as she sobbed.

"Do you want to hold him?" she asked through tears.

I took him in my arms and was immediately struck by how heavy he felt. His body was cold. He looked peaceful but didn't move. I pulled him close to me, pressed his small body to my chest, and leaned forward. I rocked back and forth with my son's body in my arms. I couldn't form a thought, much less keep one in my head.

I was lost. I handed Jayden back to Liza and held her as if for the first time.

Later that night, after Liza had gone to bed, I sat on the front porch of our home with Greg and a few friends. In a daze, I talked a mile a minute. I spoke about things I had never talked about before and haven't since. Opening a restaurant. Starting a car dealership. Learning how to play an instrument. Going to India. I couldn't control my thoughts. My son was dead.

The next several days were a blur. I couldn't escape what was happening to our family. As a man, I had to step up. There were duties I felt only I could do. I returned to the hospital the next day and arranged for the autopsy. I organized family gatherings at the house and finalized funeral arrangements.

Everyone grieves differently. Liza spent a lot of time in her room. She didn't want to see those who came to pay their respects. She just wanted to be alone. People would occasionally go upstairs and talk to her for a few minutes. I tried to accommodate everyone. I greeted people and showed them around the house. I even took several people upstairs to show them Jayden's room. Liza came out of the master bedroom and shot me an angry look.

"It's not a museum," she snapped before slamming the door behind her. She didn't want anyone in Jayden's room. She felt violated. I quickly apologized to her from behind the closed door and went back downstairs.

When Jayden died, Liza had a lot of nervous anxiety and sorrow. She would often go into the exercise room on the second floor of our house and walk for hours on the treadmill. There was a wall-mounted TV in the room. One time, a commercial for a religious artifacts store came on. At the end of the commercial, in purple ink (her favorite color), were the words "Jesus Loves You." To Liza it was a message. She was overcome with emotion and collapsed to the floor.

In the following weeks she just wasn't herself. We both struggled to communicate with one another, and I felt us drifting apart. But I couldn't let that happen. Not now. I had to be strong. I had to be the rock. Liza would, in her grief, try her best to open up.

"Why did this happen to me?" she would cry out. "Why? This is not supposed to happen. Am I really that woman who has lost a child?"

She replayed the previous months in her head. When Jayden was two months old and breastfeeding, Liza had been exhausted all the time in a way she wasn't with either Destiny or LJ.

Enjoy it, she had told herself. *This will probably be your last child. Stay in the moment no matter how tired you are.*

We buried our son on July 5, at Knolls Cemetery in Port Washington, Long Island. The funeral procession was dozens of cars long, and more than a hundred people came out to say goodbye to my son. He is laid to rest directly next to my mother, Cathy.

Jayden Joseph Odom was six months old.

In August, I returned to Los Angeles. Liza wasn't ready to leave New York, but she no longer wanted to stay in our home in Atlantic Beach. We sold the house and moved the family into an apartment in Manhattan. The first thing I did upon returning to LA was to sell our home in Marina Del Rey. I couldn't live there anymore. That's the house where Jayden was born. We kept his crib in our bedroom. I couldn't bring myself to sleep in that room anymore. His crib was still there.

I dragged the king-size mattress down the stairs and put it on the floor in the living room. I slept there for the two weeks the house was on the market. Shortly after, I moved into a house with Greg in Manhattan Beach near the Lakers practice facility.

For much of our time together as a couple Liza and I were poor communicators. When Jayden died, she shut down and what was left of our relationship began to dissolve. While she leaned on her spirituality, I turned to drugs. We never talked about my drug use. The only time I used drugs in her presence was the previous year when I took ecstasy in front of her. But now my cocaine use was beginning to spiral out of control. I was taking more than I ever had before.

I didn't want to stop. I knew I couldn't. I was three thousand miles away from my family. I sent Liza a text. It was the only time we ever talked about drugs. It read: "Cocaine will never leave me."

As you know, it was nothing for me to spend hours alone in my room. Even living in a house full of people, it didn't seem that unusual to my close friends because they knew that I needed my alone time to balance myself out. With the constant swirling drama, having a little bit of space was important to me. However, this soon became a convenient way for me to mask my drug habit. I knew no one would bother me when I locked my bedroom door.

My ability to use right under my friends' noses was significant for one huge reason—they rarely suspected or confronted me about it. I could get high in peace. I had already been suspended twice for marijuana use. The NBA's three-strike policy clearly prohibits "drugs of abuse" such as cocaine, heroin, LSD, and amphetamines, among others. Get caught with three positive tests, and one of those tests detects a hard drug, you're banned for life from playing in the NBA. You can potentially be reinstated after two years, but it's not a good look at all.

Over the years, eleven players have been banned for a prohibited substance, usually cocaine, with five eventually getting reinstated. Those who were reinstated often found little to no success upon their return.

Since my last positive drug test with the Clippers, I had used marijuana many times—daily during the summers when I knew I wouldn't be tested. I started doing coke before practices and after games when I was with the Lakers. If the league found out, my career was over at twenty-five.

One night early in the 2006–07 NBA season, my third with the Lakers, I got a call from Lakers head trainer Gary Vitti around nine.

"We got a random tomorrow," said Vitti. "Need you here at eight o'clock tomorrow morning."

Oh shit.

My heart nearly stopped.

They test you three times a year, and you never know when they're coming. I'd gamble during the season that they wouldn't test me twenty-four hours after I used cocaine, because that's how long it takes it to leave your system. I used coke about three times a week by that time. I gambled a lot. In fact, I was high at the exact moment Vitti called. That meant I had gambled one too many times. So, stop and just imagine the scenario: you're high while on the phone with the man whose job it is to tell you there's a drug test in the morning. It sounds simple, and it is if you don't use drugs, but for a drug addict it could spell the end of the world. Or at least make that potential $100 million in future earnings evaporate in ten seconds.

I hung up and told Greg that we had a problem.

"I have a random tomorrow morning, and I just took ecstasy," I told him.

"Are you sure?" he replied suspiciously. "Lamar, this is something we can't play with."

I could tell he didn't believe me, but he didn't know a thing about my cocaine habit so it's not like he could start pulling some allegations out of left field. I was scared. I thought lying could make it go away. I didn't want him or anyone to know what I was doing. Our crew had smoked weed since high school, but that was it. No one approved of hard shit. We were athletes. We didn't do that.

"Just ecstasy and weed," I lied.

There wasn't a moment to lose. We called Robbie Davis. We huddled around the computer, researching how long ecstasy stayed in your system. It lasts at least twenty-four to forty-eight hours. That was bad news.

If a player failed to show for a test, the league counted it as a positive. Three strikes and I'd be done for at least two years. I needed more help with this, so I called my agent, and we came up with a plan. We decided that there had been yet another family emergency in New York, and I had to fly there immediately. With my son's recent death, it wasn't a stretch to think we were having problems, but we had to get our story straight. Every fact had to check out down to the last detail. I called Liza and told her to keep the kids home from school. It had to look like a tragedy had occurred.

Someone called Lakers GM Mitch Kupchak to let him know that yet another great tragedy had befallen my family.

By midnight, three hours after Vitti's phone call, Greg, Robbie, and I boarded a private jet for New York. For the entire flight I drank a mix of cranberry juice and water in an effort to flush my system and get rid of all trace of the coke. We arrived in New York around five in the morning and headed for Liza's house, where I would tend to my imaginary family problem, lay low for a day or so, and be back in time for our next game.

But the NBA didn't take this lying down. A league official met me at Liza's to collect the sample.

I was nervous so it took me two hours to provide a sample. Thanks to my efforts to flush my system, my urine was as clear as water. He ran a quick test but it was inconclusive, so he needed another sample. We didn't want him waiting in the apartment, so we sent him downstairs until I was ready to pee again.

I kept drinking the cranberry concoction. Four hours later I'm ready to piss. The guy came back upstairs because of course he had to watch the sample come out of my body. At this time, the rep had been there nearly nine hours. It was a chess match, but he didn't have any moves. He hadn't eaten or even had a seat the entire time. The second time I peed it was once again as clear as water. He headed back to the league office and told them I took the test. It came back inconclusive, which at that point cleared me.

I dodged yet another bullet. One of many that would come my way.

Each of the first few years I was with the Lakers, my game and the team's success grew. And 2008 would be one of the biggest years for me personally and professionally. On February 1, 2008, one of the most significant moves in Lakers history took place. The Grizzlies traded their All-Star center, Pau Gasol, for Kwame Brown, Javaris Crittenden, Aaron Mackie, and the rights to Pau's brother, Marc. The move made the Lakers instant title contenders.

Pau was twenty-seven years old at the time, was considered the greatest member of the Memphis Grizzlies in history, and held twelve franchise records, including games played, points, rebounds, and blocked shots. The addition of Pau, alongside twenty-year-old blossoming center Andrew Bynum and myself, made the Lakers one of the longest and most versatile teams in NBA history.

We stormed to a fifty-seven-win season and finished first in the Western Conference for the first time in nearly a decade. We rampaged our way to the NBA Finals, where we played the Boston Celtics, and in the process, renewed one of the NBA's greatest rivalries. At the time, the two storied franchises had a combined thirty NBA championships. The series was one of the most competitive in years, with four of the first five games being decided by six points or less. But then Game 6 happened.

Trailing the Celtics 3–2, the bottom fell out. The Celtics' vaunted Big Three of Kevin Garnett, Paul Pierce, and Ray Allen dominated us. They were quicker to every loose ball and dominated on the boards. Allen hit a then record seven three-pointers, and point guard Rajon Rondo had a phenomenal all-around game with twenty-one points, eight rebounds, seven assists, and six blocks. The Garden crowd went berserk as the Celtics celebrated on their own floor, winning their first title in twenty-two years. We lost by thirty-nine points, the greatest deficit in NBA Finals history.

I was thrilled to finally play in the NBA Finals but also dejected by the loss. I tried to give it some perspective and realize how thankful I was to have reached the highest level of basketball. I was excited for what was to come.

It was a crashing end to a great season. The plane ride back to Los Angeles was one of the longest ever. I shut my eyes and went to sleep.

23

ate in 2008, I met the actress Taraji P. Henson at an HBO party in Hollywood. There was your typical glitz and glamour with scores of beautiful people dressed like they walked right out of the pages of a fashion magazine.

Halfway through the night, Kevin Hart came over to my table. "What's up, Lamar?" said Kevin. "I want you to meet someone."

"Who is it?" I inquired.

"Man, just trust me. It will be worth it."

I got up and walked back over to Kevin's table, where he introduced me to Taraji. We quickly struck up a conversation. Like just about every woman I met, she was more than a foot shorter than me so I had to bend way down to whisper in her ear.

She was down to earth and told me about herself—her youth in Washington, DC, her years at Howard University, what she was working on—you know, nervous small talk where both people are smiling wide, trying to feel each other out. There was just something about her. I could feel her heart was pure. She put me at ease and we hit it off immediately. To be honest, I couldn't remember where I had seen her before because I don't watch many movies, but I was too embarrassed to tell her. Then it hit me: John Singleton's 2001 movie *Baby Boy*, which was her breakout role.

We ended up exchanging numbers. Taraji was nine years older than me and had heard every line in the book. She was just such a wise woman that she could see right through whatever smooth act I was trying to put on. She refused to be just another conquest, and truthfully, I didn't want her to be. We started secretly dating and fell quickly in love. We got hot and heavy fast. It ended up being one of the happiest times of my life. Liza and I hadn't been a couple for over a year at that point. In fact, Liza respected Taraji, and we had her blessing.

Taraji got along with all my friends and could easily roll as if one of the guys. She introduced me to her fourteen-year-old son, Marcel, and was at my house nearly every day. Sometimes she'd bring some of her Hollywood friends like the actress Sanaa Lathan, who starred in *Love & Basketball*.

It was such an exciting time for both of us. The 2008–2009 Lakers stormed out of the gate and were atop the Pacific Division with a league-best 31–6 record. We were hitting our stride in what would be a season that brought the NBA title back to the city of Los Angeles after seven long years. Meanwhile Taraji was riding especially high because she had been nominated for an Academy Award for her performance in *The Curious Case of Benjamin Button*, in which she played Queenie, the adoptive mother of Brad Pitt's character.

On the night of the Golden Globes, Taraji and I went to a restaurant and had dinner with her Benjamin Button costar Brad Pitt and his wife, Angelina Jolie.

"How long have you guys been together?" asked Angelina with genuine sincerity. "It seems like you've been together forever."

I never had him pegged as a sports fan, but Brad impressed me with his knowledge of the game.

"I have a surprise for you," Taraji said to me afterward.

I had no idea what was in store as we left the restaurant and drove up into the Hollywood Hills. Destination: Prince's house.

We got there about two in the morning. When the gates opened, women set off in pairs were there to wait on the guests hand and foot. They were some of the most beautiful women I'd ever seen in LA, dressed in tight skirts and sheer black tops with their hair and makeup done perfectly. They had the kind of beauty that would intimidate even the most confident man. Everything was so tasteful and elegant. Prince was so detail oriented and spared no expense. They took our coats, brought us drinks, and directed us to a parlor in the back of the house. We passed through corridors with twenty-foot-high ceilings and white marble floors lined with massive columns like something out of Greek mythology.

When we entered the parlor there wasn't a single face I didn't recognize. We sat down and to my immediate left was Whitney Houston. Comedian Chris Tucker to the right. I tried to be cool, but I couldn't believe how close I was to Prince. The other thing that struck me was how deep his speaking voice was. It seemed strange coming from someone of such small stature.

He stood in the center of the room clutching an electric guitar. It looked so easy to him as he went through his hits and even a few songs I'd never heard before. As the night wore on, people began to shout out requests. Unable to summon the courage, I asked Taraji to request "Somewhere Here on Earth." She did so gleefully, but he didn't play it.

That night I learned how real this Hollywood stuff was, and I simply couldn't believe I was right in the middle of it.

Things were coming together, and I felt unstoppable. I was playing the best basketball of my career, the Lakers were title contenders, and I was spending every free moment with Taraji. When I find someone to love, I want to keep her by my side. But as the schedule would have it, the Lakers set out on our annual six-game Grammy road trip since the awards were being held at the Staples Center. The trip culminated with a nationally televised clash in Cleveland where I played my best game of the season, leading everyone with twenty-eight points and seventeen rebounds while my defense frustrated LeBron James into a sloppy sixteen-point performance on five for twenty shooting from the field.

But mostly, I couldn't wait to get back to Taraji. Back in LA, we hit the town as couples in Hollywood do. She introduced me to her famous friends, and I made a suitable red-carpet date. January through March is award season in Hollywood, and there was no shortage of soirees and bashes to attend.

Back out on the road a couple weeks later, the Lakers were in Minnesota on a Sunday, the night of the Oscars. It was the biggest night of Taraji's life because of her nomination for her role in *Benjamin Button*. Since I wasn't there, she brought her grandmother as her date.

We won, and I delivered twenty-five points and fourteen rebounds. After the game, there was a text message waiting for me from Taraji. It read "I didn't win."

Things were amazing, but of course I found a way to mess it up. God gave me a layup and I blew it.

About a week after dropping sixteen points and ten rebounds in a home win against the Golden State Warriors, I headed to STK, a steakhouse on La Cienega Boulevard, for teammate Luke Walton's twenty-ninth birthday. His actual birthday was about ten days away, but we were leaving for our longest road trip of the season the next morning. After setting myself up in the VIP area for a bit and watching Luke dance as goofily as humanly possible while Jordan Farmar made time with a set of dark-haired twins, I decided to set out for the SLS Hotel down the street, where I planned to meet a young woman I had made a connection with earlier in the evening.

I was back to my old ways. I felt guilty, but I was craving immediate sex. I needed to be satisfied, so I made love to a stranger for four hours. By six the next morning, I was on fumes as I called a car to take me to LAX for our 8 AM departure. I made it with minutes to spare, and to be honest, I didn't feel great about myself. I knew I was sabotaging my love life even though things were going so well.

I knew I wasn't ready to change my ways. I was twenty-nine and still hitting my prime.

24

Unlike our 2007–2008 campaign, the Lakers headed into our second consecutive NBA Finals with the league's best record and as the heavy favorite. After sailing through the Western Conference playoffs with a 12–6 record, we were to face the upstart Orlando Magic, led by star center Dwight Howard. Kobe came out cooking in Game 1, dropping forty points, eight rebounds, and eight assists, joining Michael Jordan, Shaquille O'Neal, and Jerry West as the only players to record a stat line that amazing in the NBA Finals.

Our defense smothered the Magic's inside-out offense, holding Howard to just one field goal. The rest of the series, the Magic made key adjustments and improved their ball movement, but still, we cruised to a 4–1 series victory, bringing a title back to LA.

And just like that, I was an NBA champion. It was an idea that didn't truly sink in until I went to a boxing gym about a month later, and Mike Tyson walked up to me and said, "What's up, champ?" Mike Tyson! But after the final game in the series, in the visitors' locker room, once we were done going wild during the customary champagne party, I just sat there at my locker alone, tears streaming down my face while I held the Larry O'Brien NBA Championship Trophy. I ran my fingers across the golden basketball atop the base. It was glistening from champagne. I could see my reflection in it. I held it as if I were holding a newborn. I never wanted to let it go. I was an NBA champion.

Kobe walked over to me, put his hand around my head, and embraced me. I had never seen that kind of excitement emanating from the game's best player.

"We did it! We did it," Kobe cried. "We fucking did it."

When it seemed the champagne was gone, Kobe stood in the center of the room and said, "We're gonna bring it in one time. Come on Phil, Mr. Ten."

Phil Jackson had just won his tenth championship and was hiding out in the relative safety of the trainer's room without so much as a drop of champagne on him.

"You're settled down, right?" he cautiously asked. "We're saying the Lord's Prayer, right?"

"Yeah, we're done," replied Kobe.

Of course, as soon as Phil stepped to the middle of the locker room, Kobe doused his hair with a full bottle. In about thirty seconds we must have emptied ten bottles on him. And that was back in the day before teams outfitted the players with ski goggles to prevent the champagne from stinging their eyes.

"I'm lucky," I told the cameras after I got dressed and headed for the bus. "I'm one of those people who knew what they wanted to do at nine years old. I saw myself winning an NBA championship. I'm lucky."

I was lucky indeed. And I will forever be a champion.

However, what was supposed to be one of the best days of my life was instead a haze of pain and disappointment, complete with the incessant dull pounding and stinging anxiety of a bad hit.

We arrived back in Los Angeles for a couple days of revelry before the victory parade. I partied pretty hard, but I actually couldn't tell the difference because I partied hard all the time. I guess this time it was just louder and more festive. The night before the parade, though, I stayed in, took out the coke, and invited a beautiful young lady to my house.

The next morning I was lying in my room, passed out. I have little memory of the previous twelve hours. Greg started banging on the door, saying we had to leave for the parade in an hour. All of the players had to meet at the convention center downtown to get checked in and board the bus that would take us along the parade route.

It took thirty minutes for me to muster the strength to stumble from my bed to the door. The light burned my eyes. Why was it so hot in here? I came out of the bedroom into the hallway, dizzy and sweating. Just completely out of it. Greg looked pissed. Then he stopped, furrowed his brow, and noticed something. There was blood dripping from my nose. I had done so much coke I couldn't feel my face. I thought the blood was just sweat.

"I'm not going to the parade," I said. "I can't make it. I'll just watch it on TV."

Then Greg reminded me who else was going to be there.

"What about Destiny and Lamar Jr.?" he asked. "You forget about your kids?"

Damn. I had. They had been living in LA for the last couple of years, attending elementary school. The school had given them excused absences so they could attend the parade. They were down in the kitchen having breakfast while I was upstairs bleeding from my nose. I couldn't get it together, so I sent the kids back to school. They were heartbroken.

But Greg, along with my friend Mack, who acted as my driver from time to time, wouldn't let me miss the parade even after I sent my kids away and they had to tell their teachers and classmates that their daddy was sick and couldn't go to the parade. But they had the parade on TV at the school, and there I was on the float. My kids didn't know I had gone. It looked like I just ditched them. They were embarrassed and confused and crushed.

"I thought your dad was sick?" a teacher asked them.

When I sobered up, I realized it was one of the worst things I had ever done as a father. I put my own selfish needs first. I put my beautiful, innocent children second. Now I was actually sick to my stomach with embarrassment. I just wanted to hide away from the world. Winning the championship felt like a million years ago, even though it happened a week before. I just wanted to escape from my own life. I checked into one of my favorite hotels, Shutters on the Beach in Santa Monica, blasted the AC, turned off my phone, and drew the shades tight.

I wanted to get high.

After the parade, the reality of winning the Finals and having my life change in the process was just starting to sink in. I was certainly reaping the rewards that came along with newfound worldwide attention, but I knew I was still in love with Taraji. We continued to spend a lot of time together, and she was a big part of my life, even though I wasn't being faithful to her.

Right after the Finals she told me she was going to China in July to begin filming the *Karate Kid* remake in which she had landed one of the lead roles. She would be filming for a month in several major cities as well as at the Forbidden City, the Great Wall, and the Wudang Mountains. She was adamant about me being by her side to share the experience with her.

I didn't want to go. I knew not doing so might have a big impact on our relationship, but I was still basking in the glow of a huge victory, and I didn't want to spend my summer in remote locations on the other side of the world. What if I couldn't get coke? Worse, what if Taraji discovered my habit?

She was disappointed in my decision.

To this day, I still have the same level of respect for her that I had the moment we met, and my love for her was real. She's an incredible woman from the inside out. None of her success today, from *Empire* to *Hidden Figures,* surprises me. I can't overstate her importance to black people and black culture.

I don't think I ever connected with another black woman as deeply as I did with Taraji. And to be honest, because of that fact, it hurt that much more when we broke up soon after I decided not to travel with her. As a professional athlete you're stereotyped for dating white women. Here I had this beautiful, successful, loving sister, and it gave me a sense of pride to be by her side. It's just that I met Taraji at the wrong time in my life.

Our last phone call was brief. I assured her we'd pick up right where we left off when she returned, but I could sense deep down that she knew it was over. I was deflated when we hung up because I knew I was letting a good woman get away. It was the last time I ever spoke to her.

25

During the summer of 2009, I basked in the glow of the Lakers' championship win, and newly unattached, I was highly motivated to meet women. In late August my new Lakers teammate and old friend from New York, Ron Artest, threw a welcome to Los Angeles party for himself at Halo in Hollywood. As I walked the red carpet rocking a purple shirt, with my sleeves rolled up to my elbows just how I like them, I could feel the excitement in the air.

On my arm was a beautiful young woman whom I'd known for several years. We had the kind of relationship where if either one of us needed some company or a date for an event, we were never more than a phone call away. I ran into Ron, who was looking fly in a maroon crushed-velvet blazer and sunglasses. Queens was in the building.

About an hour into the night I noticed this guy looking at me. He ventured over, probably to talk basketball or get a picture. As he got closer I realized that it was Rob Kardashian. I wasn't a big TV fan, but I knew enough to recognize him. I still remember his blue Dodgers hat, which he wore backward.

We ended up in his booth, and about an arm's length away was this woman with huge eyes. I was immediately attracted to her. We started talking and hit it off. She told me her name was Khloé. I just kept staring at her eyes and thinking how much they reminded me of my mother's. But really, I was just telling her things she'd probably heard a thousand times. And I'm just thinking: *How can I get her back to my hotel to smash?*

Hey, look, I didn't know this was going to be my wife. I didn't know I was about to fall head over heels in love. I was just doing what had always come naturally to me. She was a conquest. Apparently, she was digging me as much as I was her, and she agreed to come back to my hotel room. It took fifteen minutes to get to my room, and the whole time I was thinking that this was way too easy.

Once inside, I hopped on the bed and beckoned her to follow. She slipped off her Louboutin shoes and crawled up next to me, and we started spooning. As soon as my hands got active though, she quickly pulled away.

"What are you doing?" she asked. "I just met you."

Right away it became clear that nothing was going to happen, and I was cool with that. We talked for hours. About four in the morning, she gave me her number, called a car service, kissed me on the cheek, and left.

The next day, we made plans to meet up for dinner at Bottega Louie, an Italian restaurant in downtown LA near an apartment I kept so that I could walk to Staples Center on game days. The conversation was just as good as the night before. I quickly learned how intelligent and thoughtful she was. Unlike me, she was always on time and never missed appointments. I loved her for that and wanted those things to rub off on me. She had this endearing kind of OCD where she couldn't stand having a mess in her house and would constantly rearrange things after I unsettled them. I'm not the tidiest person in the world. It only takes about a day for my hotel room to look like a disaster area. She would put her foot down on stuff like that all the time. No other girl had ever done that with me. I thought it was sexy.

Things picked up steam in an unexpected hurry. The way our emotions, lust, spirit, and love intertwined and connected us is something I just couldn't have predicted. For the next thirty days, we scarcely left one another's side. If we did, we were texting or calling and making plans for the next time we would meet.

She introduced me to her family, and even though I had seen *Keeping Up with the Kardashians* a few times, I was taken aback at how close-knit they were. They would squabble and argue, but love always prevailed. I never had a strong family unit, and as a thirty-year-old man, it was something I still craved deeply. I'd always wanted brothers and sisters, and all of a sudden, I had five. So many holes in my life were filled instantly.

Being with Khloé made me feel like a part of the family. That was valuable to me beyond words. Being a part of Khloé's life and getting to know each member of the Kardashian family is one of the things I'm proudest of in my life. It's right up there with winning a championship and having kids.

In September 2009, Khloé and I got married. We had only been dating a month, but we both knew it was right. This was also around the time I dived even deeper into hard drugs, and my immediate group of friends had begun to go off in their own directions.

I began to see less of Greg, too. When I moved in with Khloé, it was the first time I hadn't lived with Greg since my third season with the Clippers. We continued our business relationship, but he was weary of both my drug use and the people I'd let waltz in and out of my life. We drifted apart, and even though our lives would always be connected one way or another, I rarely saw him anymore. The fact that Greg and Khloé never really warmed to each other didn't help. This was something I was blind to, and neither made an issue of it, but a rift between my friends was something that was bubbling just underneath the surface.

I overlooked and disregarded a lot of friendships when I fell in love with Khloé. My head was spinning, but that wasn't an excuse to separate myself from my friends. A lot of times this is what happens when you get married. Your world becomes smaller. There's someone new in your life who monopolizes almost all of your attention, and some people will come away with hurt feelings. I was either high or with Khloé. The cameras in my face blurred my reality.

I spent almost all of my time at our Tarzana mansion, making regular appearances on *Keeping Up with the Kardashians* and getting to know my wife. Ours was a whirlwind romance, and we were given the red-carpet treatment all over the world.

In February 2010, the New Orleans Saints were playing the Indianapolis Colts in Super Bowl XLIV. We invited a lot of our friends over to watch the game and to allow those who didn't really know each other in the first months of our marriage to hang out with one another.

Right about halftime, Greg went to the kitchen to fix a drink while Khloé was preparing a vegetable platter to take out to the main room before the halftime performance ended. Greg didn't always see eye to eye with Khloé. In hindsight, very few of my friends did. He had been with me since the beginning, while Khloé had only been around for six months, so a little power struggle was understandable.

"Hey, Greg," said Khloé, "I know you think that I'm keeping Lamar away from you guys."

"I don't think that," Greg replied.

"Just hear me out. Really. I want to tell you guys this," Khloé exclaimed. "If you think for one second that I can tell Lamar what to do, you are sadly mistaken."

Greg knew there was truth to what Khloé was saying and had no problem leaving well enough alone. But this became a recurring theme between Khloé and members of my family and close friends. I didn't really see any reason for anyone to be at odds, but our lives were changing so rapidly. I think in many ways we were still figuring out who we were becoming as people.

I knew that Khloé was my wife, and that was something that had me in a really good place. For a while, it was bliss and I was literally the happiest I've ever been in my life. We were one of the most famous couples in Hollywood, and we made more money together than we had individually at any other point in our lives. At the start of our marriage I was faithful to her. The Kardashians had the number-one-rated show on TV. I was an NBA champion, and the Lakers were barreling toward a second NBA title and third Finals appearance in a row. I felt fresh and was keeping an open mind.

The Lakers captured their sixteenth NBA title by beating the Celtics 4–3 in the 2010 NBA Finals, and although I didn't play particularly well (7.6 points and 6.6 rebounds in 7 games off the bench), I was elated to be a champion for the second time. Kobe was Finals MVP . . . again. This time I didn't do drugs the night before the parade, and I felt like my kids were proud to be by my side.

I felt inspired by Khloé to ease up on my drug use while at the same time still trying to hide it from her. When she suspected something and asked me about it, I would just shut down and go into my man cave in the basement.

But overall, I was rolling right along with a pretty positive outlook when things once again got turned upside down.

In July 2010, my cousin Curtis Smith was murdered in New York City. He was twenty-four years old. Damn, it hit me hard. Just when I thought I had escaped the dark grasp of death and finally started enjoying some sunny days, this happened. All the pain from my son's death washed up on the shore of my soul. I could barely speak at Curtis's funeral. It made me realize that because my son's death was so traumatic, so paralyzing, I never even cried. I was numb, a zombie. Curtis's death was a release. Even though they happened nearly four years apart, it was as if I was mourning two deaths at once.

When I'd come home after the season, I would drive by Curtis's projects right off FDR Drive to check on him. We'd sit on the couch and smoke and swap stories about women and life in the NBA. I'd give him whatever money I had in my pocket. He always looked on the bright side of life and had this crazy laugh. We used to call him The Star. We were incredibly close, and I felt like I lost a part of me.

While I was in New York for the funeral, I hired a car to get around the city. On a trip home from the barbershop, the car collided with a motorcycle, which then hit a fifteen-year-old boy who was walking down the street. This all happened mere blocks from where I grew up. The young boy suffered severe injuries and died the next day. At the scene of the accident I got out of the car and saw him lying on the ground. The sight of his near-lifeless body was too much to take, and I broke down crying.

I kept asking myself why this happened. Why did God take his life? What put this series of events into motion? I felt helpless—like I couldn't control the life that was happening around me. And I still had yet to say goodbye to my cousin. I prayed for that young boy for hours that night. I think about him always.

I tried my best not to backslide into drugs and fall down a familiar self-destructive spiral. Khloé was incredibly support- ive and was with me nearly every moment. I just needed time to heal. I made a decision: I would get stronger both physically and mentally. I did what I always did and buried myself in bas- ketball. Late that summer I trained in ways I never had before. I took up boxing to improve my coordination, reflexes, core, and overall endurance. I felt strong and fast. My head was clear. I was determined to have a big year on the basketball court . . . and I did. With Andrew Bynum injured to start the 2010–2011 season, I came out like a house on fire to lead the Lakers to a 13–2 record. But the season ended in a disappointing fashion as the Lakers were swept 4–0 by the Mavericks in the second round, marking the first time the Purple and Gold were swept in a playoff series in twelve years.

I set season highs of 29 points, 20 rebounds, 6 assists, and 4 blocks. After averaging 14 points, 8.7 rebounds, and 3 assists for the year, I was named the NBA's Sixth Man of the Year, which was awarded to the top reserve off the bench. It was the highest individual award I would win in my career and was incredibly cathartic. It was my All-Star Game. It was my MVP. It was me bouncing back from tragedy. I felt proud. At the press conference to receive the award I thought I could keep it together, but no, I cried.

"A lot of people don't know that Lamar Odom is the most popular player in our locker room," said Lakers general manager Mitch Kupchak to open the press conference at the Sheraton Gateway Los Angeles Hotel. "And that's not for the way he plays basketball; that's for who he is."

Khloé was in the front row taking pictures with a telephoto lens. Her mother, Kris Jenner, sat to her right and her brother, Rob, to her left. Behind her were nine of my Lakers teammates, who were happy to see me get some recognition.

"It's been a long time coming, and I've just learned so much from the dudes in my locker room," I said when I stepped to the podium. That's when I started to lose it. "I've just been blessed, but there's a couple people I just wish could be here to see [this]."

Afterward, I hugged Khloé and Kris and Pau Gasol and Luke Walton and felt loved.

Earlier that season, in January, Khloé and I started shooting our spin-off to *Keeping Up with the Kardashians* called *Khloé & Lamar*, so all of a sudden, I had two jobs. This meant we were around each other all the time, which I loved, even though it took some time getting used to the constant presence of the cameras. Whether it was with the Lakers or with Khloé, I was always at work. I had been in the spotlight for more than half of my life. Not just the spotlight, but New York and Los Angeles, the two biggest media markets in the country. But nothing could prepare me for the spotlight that came with being a member of the Kardashian family.

Even as a Laker I could move freely around town, but now that was out of the question. Paparazzi followed me to every practice, to dinners, to events. They were outside our home, in our driveway, and hiding in the bushes. I started to feel trapped and worried I wouldn't be able to handle it. That I was going to crack. I always marveled at how easily Khloé handled it all. I guess she was used to it. She gave me pep talks and told me to block out what I could. But my mind just didn't function like that.

I couldn't move in secret anymore. My drug use and infidelity were starting to pick up again, and now I had the added pressure of television cameras, telephoto lenses, and video cameras wielded by the paparazzi. I felt a measure of safety and comfort when the NBA was in season because there were a lot of places the paparazzi couldn't go, so I eagerly looked forward to getting back on the court. I was thirty-one and still had a strong ambition to make the All-Star Game. It was a life-long dream, and if it was going to happen, it needed to be the 2011–2012 season, my thirteenth.

But something unexpected and altogether different would take place.

26

I was sitting in my man cave with the lights off, thinking about the upcoming season. A lot of things were pinging back and forth through my head. I had just come off one of the best seasons of my career, and even though it was beginning to get emotionally taxing, I was still enjoying shooting *Khloé & Lamar* because it meant I got to spend all my time with my wife.

But my cocaine use had spiked in the summer of 2011, and I rarely touched a basketball all summer. I wasn't going to be in proper shape come training camp. That didn't worry me much because I knew I could ramp up my conditioning in a short window if necessary.

I'd be okay, I told myself over and over. One of my favorite things about my basement man cave was that it was one of the quietest places I could go. Khloé hardly ever came in because she knew I needed a place where I could be alone with my thoughts. I had taken up meditating to clear my head and ease the anxiety that seemed to flare up all summer.

The triggers were everywhere: my cousin's death, the demands of the show, my impending basketball mortality, the drugs, and the infidelity. The tranquility and solitude of my man cave kept me sane and allowed me to recalibrate on a daily basis. It was there in that tranquility that my world changed.

My phone buzzed, and I saw my agent's name, Jeff Schwartz, on the caller ID. I answered, and he hit me with news that blindsided me: the Lakers had traded me to the Dallas Mavericks. I asked him to repeat himself because I thought there was no way that I heard him correctly.

"I just got off the phone with Mitch Kupchak," said Jeff. "He was extremely appreciative of everything you gave this franchise, but they're going to move you."

It knocked the wind out of me. I could feel the rush of emotions rising from the pit of my stomach, but for the moment I just sat there, phone in hand, unable to speak or even form a coherent thought.

Mike Brown had recently been hired as head coach of the Lakers because Phil Jackson had retired again, and I had spoken to Brown not two weeks prior. He told me he was looking forward to working together and wanted me to keep the momentum from the last three seasons alive and well. I told him I'd been working hard that summer. I left out the part about doing cocaine the night before.

Obviously, Brown had known more about the Lakers' front office dealings than he'd let on. His voice had been upbeat, and his words were supportive, so getting traded was the last thing I was worried about. I still had a year left on my current deal and had become the first Laker to win the Sixth Man Award. I had created this false sense of security in my mind that they would never trade me because of everything I had been through during the time I had been with the organization.

My sixth-month-old son died during my second year with LA. And I was still struggling to comprehend my cousin's

death. Everyone in the organization was incredibly supportive. Factoring in my role as a cornerstone of two championship teams, I fooled myself into thinking I had accrued enough
goodwill to be untradeable. I thought I was going to be a Laker
for the rest of my career. Los Angeles was my second home.
The organization was my family. I was going to retire a Laker.

I was very wrong.

The trade destroyed me mentally, and I could see the most
miserable, least productive year of my career barreling down
on me like a runaway freight train. Even if I had been in shape
and sober, I still wouldn't have been able to give the Mavericks anything. My love for the game vanished into thin air. My
competitive nature faded like day disappearing into night, and
there wasn't a positive thought in my head.

I was also underweight, stressed out, and self-medicated.

I didn't want anything to do with the Lakers either, and
that was a strange feeling because that franchise was my life.
I was consumed with anger. Mitch Kupchak, who was sing-
ing my praises at the Sixth Man press conference five months
earlier, didn't even call to let me know. I loved my teammates,
but I didn't want to speak to them. It would only make the hurt
worse.

When I arrived in Dallas, my first conversation with Mavericks
owner Mark Cuban was fairly routine.

"Lamar, we're really excited to have you," said Cuban.
"You're coming off a great year and will be a big part of what

we do. I can't wait to see you and Dirk [Nowitzki] on the court together."

It was really just jerk-you-off bullshit. I was as professional and cordial as I could possibly be, but I was already planning my escape. I simply did not want to be in Dallas. My mind was in such a funk, I knew I was never going to recover. I had to go about the normal routine of arriving in a new city despite the fact I was in a haze. Meet my new teammates. Greet season ticketholders. Learn the playbook. Find a place to live. Do interviews. On top of that, I had my obligation to *Khloé & Lamar*.

But I was honest and told Cuban I was in a bad place mentally.

"I'm not doing well right now," I said. "God has just dealt me so much that it's hard to take. I'm not dealing with it."

"We'll take care of you and support you as best we can," replied Cuban. "This is a family down here."

The lockout-shortened 2011–2012 season was a lost cause for me on the court. I played poorly from the first tip-off to the final horn. I could never put together two consecutive good games. Hell, I had a hard time putting together a good quarter. I didn't hustle. I barely boxed out. I'd just hope the days and weeks would fly by.

That wasn't even the worst part. Cuban quickly grew to resent me; it seemed his goal was to make my time in Dallas as miserable as possible. He rode me constantly, talked down to me, and questioned my manhood in front of others. During home games he'd grab his usual courtside perch and proceed to hurl obscenities at me.

"You're so fucking slow and out of shape," Cuban screamed at me during a dead ball situation early in my ill-fated tenure with the Mavs. "Waste of fucking money."

"What the fuck are you doing?"

"Hustle, dammit!"

"This is just awful."

The owner of the team was *heckling* me. He was cursing me out in front of fans and players. It said "Dallas" on my chest. *I play for you, asshole!* Would Jerry Buss, owner of the Lakers, ever do something like this? Would any decent human? And the players on my new team, guys I barely knew, were watching all of this play out. I had no idea what they thought of me. But how could they possibly respect me if I didn't stand up for myself?

I searched for answers anywhere I could. Was he hating on me because the Lakers used to kick their ass? Was it the reality show? Was I actually *that* bad?

I wanted to lash out. I had fantasies of just walking up to him and sucker-punching him. I needed to take my aggression out, but I kept it as cordial as possible whenever we were on the team plane or in the locker room. I'd give him a half smile and my least threatening voice. I had to placate him. Convince him I wasn't a physical threat. Because I wasn't going to win if I went down that path. But apparently, he didn't have any problem being physical with me.

During one homestand, I was having possibly the worst game of the season. Head Coach Rick Carlisle subbed me out, and I looked for a seat near the coaches, but none were available. So I went down to the only open seat at the end of the bench. Right next to Cuban.

Cuban extended his right foot and kicked my shin. "Come on, motherfucker!" he shouted.

I was stunned. This wasn't a tap. I felt it. That was the last straw. It was painfully clear he did not respect me as a man. I felt the adrenaline rush through my body. In an instant I was transported back to Linden Boulevard, where the slightest act of disrespect could be fatal. As I sprang up, Vince Carter, who was sitting next to me, grabbed my arm tightly and leaned in.

"LO, chill out," Vince calmly said. "Don't do it. It's not worth it."

A physical confrontation with Cuban would have been the end of my career—a dark moment that I would have been remembered for despite being a two-time NBA champion.

What if Vince, who I had the closest connection to on that team, hadn't been sitting there? What if he had been paying attention to the game and hadn't seen the incident? I can say beyond a shadow of a doubt that Vince Carter saved me from catching a charge and ending my career in disgrace.

As I slogged through the season, absorbing one slight and disrespectful act after another, Cuban would deal me one final indignity just because he could. On March 2, I was assigned to the Texas Legends, which was the Mavericks' D-League affiliate. A roster spot on the Legends was generally meant for NBA hopefuls on the fringe of the league who the Mavs deemed worthy of development. It was an alternative to playing in Europe. It was a place where players made an average of $14,000 for the entire season.

The move was solely meant to humiliate me. Hell, no, I wasn't going to do it. That would have meant I went from Sixth Man to the D-League in less than nine months. I would rather retire. A day later, I was recalled without playing a game for the Legends.

On March 24, during a 104–87 loss to the San Antonio Spurs, I got my first DNP-CD (did not play—coach's decision) of my career.

Things came to a head on April 7 in Memphis. We were in the locker room at halftime. I had played four scoreless minutes in the first half. Cuban had been hounding me all game, and he stormed into the locker room, got up in my face, and angrily screamed at me in front of the team, asking me if I was "in or out."

I didn't take kindly to it. Once again, he didn't treat me like a man. That's not how you handle something in front of the entire team. Man, it was heated. I had fantasies about decking him, but that wasn't the way out. I never played another game for the Mavs.

Here's what Cuban told ESPN:

Everybody goes through ups and downs. Every player does. We tried to put him in a position to succeed. You guys saw it, saw what we did. It didn't work. And I just asked him, does he want to go for it or not? Is he in or is he out? I think he thought we were playing poker. I just didn't get a commitment. And that was the end. My job is to look at every player, employee, whatever and just treat them individually and put them in a position to succeed. I've failed miserably on this one. It's not the first time and won't

be the last time. Move on to the next. Did I get my money's
worth? No. I don't know that the word's "cheated." But did I get
my money's worth? No.

Real nice.

In the end I averaged career lows in points (6.6), rebounds
(4.7), assists (1.7), and field-goal percentage (35.2).

On June 29, the Mavericks dealt me to the Clippers as part
of a four-team trade. At the very least, the worst chapter of my
basketball life was over. But my downward spiral would only
pick up steam. I was about to spin out of control.

27

Khloé and I moved back to Los Angeles after our year in Dallas. I was back with the Clippers, where it all started. Head Coach Doc Rivers welcomed me with open arms. He had always been friendly and kind to me. I would play a full eighty-two games despite my rapidly accelerating drug use and weakened body, but I knew my career was over. I didn't know if Doc knew, but I did my best to hide my lethargy. We were finishing the second season of *Khloé & Lamar* on E! and I was at my wits' end.

I could not handle the potentially lethal cocktail of the spotlight, drug addiction, a diminishing basketball career, and infidelity. Oh, did I mention the paranoia, anxiety, depression, hangovers, withdrawal, and rejection? But back to the infidelity . . . I struggled to remain faithful. I couldn't keep my dick in my pants or the coke out of my nose.

My man cave had huge custom-made leather chairs, thick brown carpeting, and a cigar bar. Man, I loved that room. But it was also where so many of my demons lived.

Drug addicts are incredibly skilled at hiding their habit. It starts with the lies and deception. I'd get defensive all the time and Khloé would just drop it. It's easy to hide the activity, but far more difficult to hide the hangover, weight loss, and manic behavior.

I'd be down in my cave snorting insane amounts of coke, waiting for my dick to get hard like that first time at the Shore Club in Miami seven years ago. Then I'd run upstairs to the bedroom, where Khloé was waiting. She didn't ask any questions. I'd always hit the lights and take care of business.

One day she got tired of waiting and came downstairs looking for me. I had done a couple hits but hadn't left the cave. She banged on the door. I didn't respond.

"What are you doing in there?" said Khloé. "Come out. Now."

After an hour or so she became concerned but didn't want to call the police. So she called Greg. She only ever called Greg in an emergency. He arrived an hour later with Alex Harris.

"He's acting crazy," Khloé said. "He's hallucinating. He's saying people are trying to kill him."

At that point I couldn't tell reality from fantasy. I was on ecstasy and coke. I was sure that people were coming for me. They wanted to get me. They were listening to everything I was saying. They could read my thoughts. They were in my phone. They were in my head. They were in the walls.

"Who put these fucking mikes in my wall!" I screamed. "Why are you following me?"

I took a golf club and swung away. I began smashing the walls to find them. I was convinced they were in there. I just kept swinging and ripping out the drywall. "I'm gonna fucking find you!" I screamed. "This is my fucking house. I'll get you lying motherfuckers!"

I had knives. I would kill them before they killed me. Before I was done there were dozens of gaping holes in the walls. The golf club was bent in half. My hands were bloody from ripping out the walls. Khloé was hysterical and had dashed up to the bedroom and shut the door. I was exhausted. I hadn't slept in thirty-six hours.

I stumbled over to the door and slumped to the ground with my back up against the door. I did some more coke. At this point I was just putting it in my hand and shoveling it in my nose. The coke was everywhere. I would have eaten it if I thought it would get me higher.

Then . . . a knock on the door.

"Yo, Money, what are you doing in there?" Greg said. He kept banging on the door. I thought if I sat perfectly still he would think I was gone and just leave. I waited for fifteen minutes.

"Lamar, what's good? Open the door," he said. I texted him despite being only inches away.

"Yo what up? Just chillin at my house," I wrote. Every time he asked a question, I texted him back. I could hear Greg and Alex talking, confused by my behavior.

After a half hour of this back-and-forth, Greg and Alex went to the kitchen and Khloé came down and knocked on the door. I opened it suddenly and grabbed her forcefully by the shoulders, which frightened her.

"What the fuck are you doing?" I screamed, out of my mind. "You trying to embarrass me in front of my friends? I'll fucking kill you! You don't know what I'm capable of!" She ran back upstairs and I slammed the door.

After two hours, Greg and Alex left. As I came down from my high, the paranoia wore off, and I asked Khloé to forgive me. I was embarrassed and ashamed. It was a new low for our relationship and for my life . . . the most regrettable moment in a series of regrettable moments.

Khloé knows now I have a drug problem, I thought.

Things were quiet for the rest of the day, with Khloé and I in separate rooms. The silence was deafening. For the first time I realized that this thing could kill me and that I was capable of hurting the people I loved. I went to sleep, praying for a cure.

Infidelity had become a regular part of my life. I had broken my vows with Khloé so many times it's just impossible for me to remember them all. Each time I was doing wrong and I knew it. I don't know why Khloé stayed with me. She couldn't trust me at all. I couldn't trust myself either. I'd always find some self-important way to justify my actions. Khloé would get wise and become ever more vigilant in uncovering my cheating ways. She started checking my Black Card statements. She tracked my movements when she saw a charge pop up, usually a hotel or some kind of bottle service. That's how she found me at the legendary Hotel Roosevelt in Hollywood that night in 2012.

I had arranged for two strippers to meet me there for an indefinite stay. I reached out to my drug contact and had a nice little stash of weed that would last me a few days. When the girls showed up, they had their own supply, so we laid everything out on a coffee table in neat little piles. Meanwhile, Khloé was frantically calling and texting me. She saw the charge and had a pretty good hunch what I was doing. I wasn't yet hip to her new sleuthing method, so the idea of her finding me was the last thing on my mind.

The girls called other girls to come over to do blow and fuck, and I didn't mind at all. Around midnight I heard a pounding on the door. I got up and looked through the peephole, shocked to see Khloé, Kris Jenner, and their security team in the hallway. They had asked the front desk what room I was in because that information didn't show up on the credit card statement. The front desk gave them a key card to my room. There were naked girls everywhere. Khloé opened the door and pounced on the first girl she saw. That's when her security bulldozed the door and rushed into my den of iniquity. Try to imagine the scene: Khloé's beating the shit out of one of the girls who tried to protest. She's dropping vicious blows all over the top of this girl's head. Kris is screaming and her security guard jumps in and pulls Khloé off the beaten stripper. Khloé tells me to gather up my things, and the guards quickly remove all traces of the drugs. We sneak out of a back door of the Roosevelt and disappear into the night.

I first met Jamie Sangouthai at Christ the King. We were in the same grade, and he even had a stint on the end of the bench on the basketball team. He was quick with a joke and had that trademark Queens edge to him, and even though we weren't that close in high school, I always liked him. I had rarely seen him since we graduated high school in 1997, but when the

Heat advanced to the playoffs in 2004, my first time in the post-season, I wanted to celebrate by flying in my old friends from Queens. He had gone to school to study information technology and ended up working on Wall Street for a while.

Jamie was an Italian kid from Queens who may not have been long on talent, but he had a good heart and I trusted him. He had dreams of making it in Hollywood as a record producer, and it felt good to reconnect with him.

In 2008, during my time with the Lakers, Jamie moved out to Los Angeles to follow his show business dreams. I put him up in a two-thousand-square-foot loft next door to mine at the Roosevelt Lofts, four blocks from Staples Center. And I got him a nice car, which didn't go over well with a lot of my friends who had been out here with me since the early Clippers days. It was understandable that guys might be a little territorial, but I just wanted everyone to get along and enjoy the ride we were on.

Jamie ended up starring on *Khloé & Lamar* as my best friend. My boys were pissed about that because he had just showed up. They knew he wasn't my best friend, but the producers needed someone who was white. My longtime black friends hated that, while I just went along with it.

Another reason his presence didn't go over well was because it quickly became apparent that Jamie had a penchant for hard drugs, which was a no-no with my immediate crew. I already had extensive experience with cocaine, but none of my friends knew about it at that point. And Jamie was hard-core. He used needles and was constantly on the lookout for heroin.

Even though he didn't have much Hollywood know-how, he was ambitious, and I wanted to help. He had an idea for an upscale menswear clothing line called Take Out. I connected him with a few folks in fashion, and he networked as best he could. Several people told me not to go into business with him, but if I didn't help him, who would?

I was also hell-bent on starting a record label, and thought Jamie, with his charm, street sense, and bravado, was the perfect fit to run it.

In November 2008, I had gone to the GQ Men of the Year party at the famed Chateau Marmont on Sunset Boulevard. It was a black-tie who's who of famous faces all sipping drinks and nibbling on finger snacks on the garden terrace beneath the stars. I stood in a tight circle with Justin Timberlake, the rapper T.I., and Jay-Z as we made small talk and discussed what upcoming projects we had in the works.

"I got an idea for a record label I'm about to start up," I told Jay-Z excitedly. He shook his head.

"Don't do it," he warned. "Put your money in real estate. All the money is taken here."

T.I. started to laugh. "He ain't lying, LO."

I thought Jay was trying to play me because he didn't want me creeping into his lane. New Yorkers were supposed to be supportive of one another, but Jay was dismissive. He wasn't rude about it, but he was far from encouraging and didn't offer any advice or connects.

I decided to go ahead with the project under my fledgling brand, Rich Soil, which I first started as a T-shirt line that represented growth and prosperity. I put Jamie in charge of the label, and he got to work right away. He hired a small staff, began meeting with A&R people, created marketing campaigns, and searched for unsigned acts online and in studios around town.

From the outside, things looked like a well-oiled burgeoning enterprise. But looks can be deceiving. I spent $500,000 on a Rich Soil promotional event in Miami on Memorial Day weekend before we had signed a single artist. We were booking first-class tickets and five-room suites in whatever city we visited.

If the record label wasn't hemorrhaging money, it was burning it. And whatever was left was flushed down the toilet. All told, I lost nearly $8 million without putting out so much as a single album. Soon after, Take Out went under because we couldn't secure outside funding. Ultimately, Jamie was in over his head. It was my mistake to put someone in charge of a record label and fashion line who had no experience running either.

We made a hell of a splash, threw great parties, and looked every bit the part. We just never made any music. I should have listened to Jay-Z. Here I thought he was trying to play me, and he was really trying to help me.

I regularly did hard drugs with Jamie back in Miami. That's how Scott Storch and I crossed paths. I didn't want to admit it, but I kept Jamie around because he was my go-to enabler. He had easy access to crack and heroin and was always finding harder drugs to try. Having him tucked away downtown where none of my friends lived or interacted with him helped me cover my tracks.

While I was on one bender or another, Jamie was doing the same. By 2015, no longer a reality TV star, he was strung out, desperate, and broke. And on June 14, he died before he wanted to.

A bacterial skin infection crept into his body and killed him. It was from his heroin addiction. Another light that went out.

had been texting and talking with Khloé all day. But by September 2015, we were in the middle of a divorce. Sometimes the conversation was civil, at others, it was tense. Then there were the calls where we just screamed at each other. Crying, yelling, cussing. There was so much anger. We were looking for a love that had long passed and was never coming back. We were chasing something that no longer existed. I was renting a house in Las Vegas in order to get back in shape, and it was as hot as you want it to be in September. Liza and the kids were still in New York, and I rarely saw them during my marriage to Khloe.

I wanted one last run at the NBA. I had lost thirty pounds, and even though my body was getting stronger, I still felt like I was losing control. My mind was fragile. My confidence was low, and I didn't feel like myself. People told me I looked good, but I didn't take it as a compliment. It just felt like pity.

With each call or text from Khloé, I felt like I was starting to unravel a little more. I tried to unwind by hitting one of my favorite spots, a restaurant called Cleo at the SLS Las Vegas, to let off some steam with my friends. I took a table in a dark corner at the back of the restaurant and ordered a cognac. Khloé hadn't texted for an hour, and I tried not to think about it as I savored my drink. I wanted my mind to be anywhere but on what caused me the most pain at the moment.

I thought about my sophomore year at Christ the King. I had thirty-six points in the City Title game. That was the first time anyone ever heard of Lamar Odom.

I thought about Mildred Mercer. I still can't believe God blessed me with a grandmother with such grace, beauty, and strength. She took me from a boy to a man. I owed my life to her. When I was twelve she said something that I carry with me to this day. I didn't understand it then, but it has come to define my life.

"What you do in the darkness comes out in the light."

From the darkness to the light.

In the back of the dark restaurant my phone buzzed and glowed. It was Khloé. I knew if I answered, it would lead to another fight. I felt like our entire relationship was hanging in the balance. I had hurt her and I was hurt, but I felt betrayed more than anything. The people I loved had thrown me away. I know I wasn't perfect. Far from it. I had a hand in this mess, too. It's not easy to be with someone with habits like mine. I told my friends in that restaurant how I would do anything for that family. Not just for Khloé but for Kris, Rob, Caitlyn, Kim, Kourtney, Kendall, and Kylie. Now they didn't want me around. Well, mostly Kris. So, Khloé by extension. Kris was only interested in protecting the Kardashian brand, which was an international phenomenon. She was the matriarch and guardian of a massive empire and the hundreds of millions of dollars it generated. It was always about her brand. I was nothing to her.

Kris called me later that night to tell me that Khloé wanted to speak to me in person the next day in LA. Khloé had gone dark after her last text, an hour or so before, so I assumed she had fallen asleep. I hadn't seen her for a couple weeks, so I didn't hesitate to go to Los Angeles. Actually, I couldn't wait, so I left in the middle of the night. I didn't even pack a change of clothes. I called my driver, George, and we headed down the I-15 freeway from Vegas for the three-and-a-half-hour drive to Los Angeles.

I was high on cocaine, weed, and alcohol. I was dead tired and wired all at once. I tried to sleep but I couldn't. We did ninety miles an hour all the way, yet it felt like the drive took forever. But it still wasn't enough time to find the right words to say to Khloé. I searched all night for the perfect words and they never came. I hated her and loved her all at once. I could kiss her and curse her in the same breath. But I was desperate to talk to her. I knew this was my last chance.

Kris said Khloé would be at SoulCycle in Beverly Hills at 6 AM, and she was right on time. As she walked down the sidewalk dressed in her workout clothes, I jogged across the street to say hello.

"Khloé," I called out.

She stopped in her tracks. Right away I knew something wasn't right.

"What are you doing here, Lamar?" she asked with a stunned expression. "I don't want to see you."

"I just drove all the way from fucking Vegas like you said. What are you talking about?"

She sidestepped me, and I stopped in front of her, begging to talk. I instinctively reached out to grab her arm. She pulled back quickly.

I was completely confused. I wasn't even high anymore. I was anxious and agitated, but I had come down from the high. It all felt like a movie I didn't want to be in.

What the fuck is going on? I thought to myself. Then I saw the first camera. Then another. Still more.

As much as the paparazzi followed me around, invaded my privacy, and made my life a living hell, I was certain of one thing: there was no way they could have known I was going to be at SoulCycle in Beverly Hills at six o'clock in the morning on a Saturday.

Well, actually, there was one way. Laugh out loud.

It had to be Kris. She must have called the paparazzi and arranged for them to be there, knowing Khloé would be caught off guard and react accordingly. Now here's the kicker—and this will show you how devious Kris Jenner is—Khloé had no idea I was going to be there. She was frightened and jittery. From the outset it looked like I was ambushing her while she walked to her workout. We were on bad terms and she didn't want me there. It all began to make sense.

When I realized what had happened, my rage started to boil. I was about to lose control. The cameras caught the entire encounter on tape. There had been a sliver of hope for us to reconcile. I wanted to get back together. Kris knew this was my last chance, but she didn't want a drug addict in the family. It wasn't good for business. Any chance I had left with Khloé exploded on the spot.

For some reason, as pissed off as I was at the paparazzi, I decided to give them an interview right there on the street. I even agreed to be miked up. I told you I wasn't in my right mind. My head was cloudy as I rambled, angry and desperate. I was broken. I knew I was doing the wrong thing by talking, but I couldn't stop myself.

I was sweating and pacing. I was still wearing the same black sweat suit from the night before. I said:

I don't believe in what y'all do. I don't believe in following people around. Even if half the things were true, people know who I am. And y'all have discredited me, beat me down, took my confidence, took everything away from me. You will not do it again.

I was one step closer to rock bottom. One step closer to death.

Two days later I returned to Las Vegas to get back to my work-outs and get my mind off what happened with Khloé. I still wanted to play in the NBA, and my summer workouts were paying off. But the incident with Khloé had shaken me. My mind was swimming, and I needed the pain to go away. So, I did it the only way I knew how.

I decided to get away just for a weekend or so. My driver was in Los Angeles handling business. Greg was in Mexico on his honeymoon with his new wife, Eve. I was by myself. This made it easy for me to sneak off for a weekend getaway.

After all, I thought, I deserved it. I was doing well. I was working out. I was in the best shape since my playing days with the Lakers. And I was staying out of trouble with the law. Aside from the incident with Khloé, I had kept a low profile.

I decided to spend the weekend at the Love Ranch, a well-known desert brothel about ninety minutes from my house in Las Vegas. I packed an overnight bag and grabbed my American Express Black Card and a $25,000 wad of cash. The Ranch even sent me a driver.

As the car barreled down Interstate 160, bringing me closer to the end of my life, I thought about turning around. I looked out of the window as we got farther from the bright lights, and the barren, cold desert flew by. I had plenty of time to stop the car. To try to make things right. But I didn't. I couldn't.

And this is the truly sad part. I was giving up. As we floated down that highway—a stranger from the Love Ranch behind the wheel—I was giving up on my NBA career. I regret it to this day. I turned my back on the only thing that ever gave me solace. Training camps had started two weeks ago, and nobody called me. I held out hope that someone would offer me a ten-day contract. While the rest of the league was going through conditioning drills, learning new defenses, and perfecting their footwork, I was destroying my mind and my body.

It's funny how much of my trouble has come down to drugs and women. The number of days that blended into nights that I spent with a beautiful woman and a mound of drugs.

My getaway weekend would be no different.

We pulled off the highway and the driver steered the vehicle onto a dirt road that led to the brothel. The place didn't look like much. There was almost nothing there. A dirt-rock desert, a couple power lines, and mountains off in the distance. You know you're there when you see the crummy red-and-yellow sign leading up to the place boasting that they're "Always Open" and "Always Tasty." The bottom of the sign informs you "No Sex Required."

The buildings are low-slung, one-story beige units that look like the world's most isolated trailer park. I jumped out and headed for the compound's main building, which had a bright red front door. I was greeted by the property manager.

I arrived on a Saturday night and was pretty loaded and needed to sleep it off. So the first night I just crashed. The next day I wanted to mingle. I walked through the complex and exchanged pleasantries with most of the staff and met the girls who worked there. The vibe was laid-back and welcoming. I already had my eye on who I wanted to entertain me that night, but the only thing I could think about was food. I couldn't remember the last time I ate. I didn't want to eat alone so I ordered $500 worth of Kentucky Fried Chicken for the whole place.

After lunch I went to the bar and ordered a bottle of cognac to loosen up. On Monday, my third day there, I needed to be alone. I slept most of the day and into the night.

About twelve hours later, on Tuesday morning, my body was convulsing.

I lay on the floor, dying.

I had finally killed myself.

Maybe I wanted this, but that wasn't important. The women who kept me company screamed and called 911. No one was strong enough to pick me up. My face was pressed against the floor. Blood ran from my nose and mouth. I have little recollection of what happened that day because I had lost consciousness sometime that morning. I've had to rely on the accounts of friends and family and employees of the Love Ranch.

I was taken to the hospital and delivered to a bed in room 228 at Sunrise Hospital in Las Vegas. My heart had stopped twice. I had twelve seizures and six strokes. My lungs collapsed and my kidneys ruptured. There were tubes going every which way, and I was on life support. Everyone I'd ever loved was looking at me through bleary eyes. I wanted to touch them. Kiss them. I wanted to say I'm sorry.

But I couldn't. Because I wasn't alive.

I stared at God. He stared right back at me.

The preacher man walked out into the hallway. My family started to cry.

I'm an addict. I *was* an addict. My coma is the completion of my addiction. It is the completion of my life. The end of my spiral, anxiety, pain, frustration, confusion, and lethal self-medication.

This is the final portrait of Lamar. Fuck. I'm not ready.

Today is the day I'm going to die.

Tell Lamar Jr. and Destiny I love them. I cannot. It wasn't my plan, but I'm done. I'm scared. I'm empty. There is nowhere else for me to turn. I've had an answer for everything my whole life. It was part of what made me Lamar Joseph Odom. I've always had the answer. Queens raised me, after all. Its grit, heart, and passion flowed in my veins. The pulse of the broken, beautiful streets made my heart burst. Gave me the skill to survive, which kept me alive for thirty-five years. But that's over now. There is no direction in which I can turn. There are no more happy endings. No more pretty girls. No more luck or good fortune. No more answers.

There is an unholy concoction of cocaine, cognac, and cannabis coursing through my veins. I bet against my demons and they won. They have conspired to stop the heart in my six-foot-ten, 256-pound body.

I am no longer in control of my life. I am a slave to everything I hate.

I am powerless. Damn. I never thought I'd say that.

My children are all I have left. Their beautiful faces, the soft touch of their skin is tattooed on my mind. The melody of their voices plays like a symphony. I want to reach out to them but they're not here. I am alone. It's time for me to leave this world. I tried. I really did. But I am not strong. I have no more love to give.

The hospital was put on lockdown. Before anyone knew it, word of my life-and-death struggle had spread like wildfire over social media, and the hospital was swarming with paparazzi, tourists, and curious onlookers. The staff cleared out an entire wing on the second floor and posted a security guard outside the elevator.

I was surrounded by a team of doctors who monitored my vital signs around the clock. A ventilator helped me breathe while a feeding tube was inserted in my abdomen. With all the electrodes attached to my head to monitor my brain activity, I'm sure I looked like something out of a science-fiction movie.

As I lay in room 228 behind a glass wall designed to keep germs out while allowing doctors a clear view of me, I had no idea of the chaos that was beginning to swirl around me. And none of it had anything to do with hospital equipment or frantic nurses. A force of nature was on its way: Khloé Alexandra Kardashian. To say her arrival would kick things up a notch is an understatement.

There was pure bedlam in the first-floor lobby, which doubled as a de facto waiting area—eventually spilling into the emergency room—for the crush of people who came to see me. Several hours after I was admitted, still completely unconscious, family members and friends began to arrive from all over the country. Everyone was told to wait and was given very little information. Security was tighter than any club I had ever been to.

Khloé took control.

The only people she allowed upstairs in those early hours as my life hung in the balance were her best friend, Malika Haqq; Greg; and our mutual friend Alex. Since the judge had not yet signed off on our divorce papers, Khloé and I were technically still married. That meant she controlled everything during my Vegas hospital stay. I mean everything. She was in charge of all medical decisions and was the primary contact point for the doctors who delivered constant updates. She tightly guarded access to my second-floor ward and decided who was allowed to enter the room.

The officers from the Nye County Sheriff's Office were the one group she couldn't rebuff. After interviewing the girls who worked at the Love Ranch, they suspected I was using drugs and showed up with a warrant to collect a blood sample. As I lay unconscious, they wanted evidence to charge me with a crime. So much for compassion. What's a coma, give or take?

Khloé also made an exception for my former Lakers teammate Kobe Bryant and Lakers GM Mitch Kupchak. I never had a teammate I admired as much as Kobe. And Mitch, well, he made my Laker dreams come true by arranging a trade with the Miami Heat to bring me to LA in 2004. They snuck out of the MGM Grand Garden Arena three miles away during the third quarter of a preseason game with the Sacramento Kings to be by my side. The team told the media Kobe had a leg contusion.

At this point the phones were lighting up around the country. Khloé stood next to my bed trying to organize trips to the hospital for loved ones while keeping them informed. Then she called her mom, explaining the situation through tears.

"I have no idea what's going on," she said frantically into the phone. "The doctors are running all these tests and still can't figure out why he's in a coma. Where are you?"

Friends from Vegas, New York, and Los Angeles were desperately trying to get details about what happened while arranging flights to McCarran International Airport.

Several hours later, the rest of the cavalry finally arrived. Kris Jenner, Kim Kardashian, and Kylie Jenner made their way past throngs of family and friends and well-wishers crammed like sardines in the lobby.

Out front, media trucks lined the streets. Reporters from across the country did live feeds and turned over every rock for a scoop. Helicopters swirled above. The sound of their blades chopping the air was the background music of my fight to live. Kevin Frazier from *Entertainment Tonight* tried to win family members over with free fried chicken in hopes of getting an exclusive. Paparazzi tried to climb up service ladders to gain access to the roof. Someone even flew a drone outside my window.

The tension only worsened after the rest of the Kardashians arrived. I had cousins and childhood friends waiting for hours who got bumped out of line by my famous sisters-in-law. Obviously, I had no idea what was going on. This was Khloé's call, and she had never even met most of my family. As far as she was concerned, they were strangers. It was starting to get rowdy on the first floor, and my loved ones' anxiety and frustration were on the brink of boiling over. People in the lobby saw Instagram posts that said Kobe and Mitch were allowed in through a side door, and that caused stress levels to rise even higher.

"It was getting real nasty downstairs," Greg would tell me months later while trying to piece together the week for me. "They wanted to know who was calling the shots."

Meanwhile the tension in my hospital suite on the other side of the glass partition wasn't any better. Aunt JaNean arrived with Destiny and Lamar Jr., who were seventeen and thirteen at the time. JaNean was tired from her flight and in no mood to deal with any shot callers, whether I was married to one of them or not. She had never met any of the Kardashians before. She was from Queens and was not easily impressed. When she entered the room, Kim and Khloé stopped what they were doing and looked up at her.

"Y'all ain't that cute," said Aunt JaNean dismissively. "You're cuter on TV."

The Kardashians sat in stunned silence, looking at each other. There wasn't any comeback for that. Kim's and Khloé's faces said it all: *What the fuck just happened?* Plus, I know my aunt, and if they *had* responded, the room would have exploded. Khloé knew enough not to say anything, and it just isn't in Kim's nature. Though they were sitting right next to each other, they started texting back and forth furiously.

JaNean took my kids in to see me, and the doctors informed them that I could likely hear them but was unable to respond. I was told they had tears streaming down their faces. They were devastated to see their father like this. It's probably a good thing I couldn't see them; the heartbreak would have been too much to bear. But something special happened in that room right then. Their voices gave me strength. I could feel their heartbeats in sync with mine. The life was coming back to my body.

After Destiny and Lamar Jr. left my hospital room on the second night of my stay, Greg took them to an adjacent waiting room. Everyone was raw with emotion and trying to catch their breath. And that's precisely when everything hit the fan. When JaNean left my room, she went to the waiting area on the other side of the glass partition and took an open seat: the very seat Kris Jenner had been sitting in for hours. When Kris got back from the restroom, she approached JaNean.

"That's my seat," said Kris.

"No, it isn't," replied JaNean. "This is my seat now, thank you."

Khloé tried to take control. She wanted Aunt JaNean to leave the room. Bad idea.

"Y'all not his family!" Aunt JaNean shouted. "We're his family!"

The Queens in her came out and she let off a stream of expletives. The situation was about to go off the rails, but Greg was able to usher JaNean to the nearby room where Destiny and Lamar Jr. were waiting. The "fuck yous" and "bitches" were flying in every direction. People had actually forgotten why they were there: because I was barely cling-ing to life. Khloé started working the phones and then met with her security. She wanted everyone who entered the room to sign nondisclosure agreements, which meant no one could talk or write about what they saw. In the middle of the chaos, they were still trying to protect their brand. My family refused to sign. When everybody balked, Khloé fumed and locked down the second floor. She added more security by the elevators and cut off all visitation. The thirty-five people downstairs had no shot to see me. Even my father, who I had just repaired a thirty-year broken relationship with, was only allowed in once.

But Khloé never left my side. She didn't shower for four days and brushed her teeth in a small room next door. Kim's resilience was incredible, too. She was seven months pregnant with her second child. They would put three chairs together for her to sleep across at night.

Even with all the ramped-up security, civil rights leader Jesse Jackson managed to make his way up to see me. He was initially denied entry by Khloé's security, but after he said he wanted to pray with me, Khloé let him in. Jesse took my hand and said a prayer over my unconscious body.

Afterward, Khloé specifically asked him to avoid the media. She wanted to maintain control of all information going in and out of the room. She clung to control the narrative of my impending death like only she could. She implored Jackson to respect the family's privacy.

Jesse left the hospital and promptly held a press conference. Khloé was furious. My friends essentially disowned Jackson. Everyone felt betrayed.

"Khloé is by his side," Jackson told the slew of cameras. "He is unconscious but apparently the doctors say he is recovering. I don't know how long it will take. He is in a very difficult situation. I can only pray for his recovery. But at least there is some responsiveness now. Yesterday he was almost totally unresponsive and today there are some signs of responsiveness. We just held hands and I'm hoping he will bounce back. I don't want to use the term critical or stable, but it looks critical to me. But he's surrounded by love and I'm sure it was a joy to the family that Kobe stopped by."

My vitals had only slightly improved by the third day in intensive care, and I was nowhere near out of the woods. The prevailing thought was that if I didn't recover soon, I'd have severe brain damage and limited ability to speak, walk, or function in any way. The best-case scenario that was floated to my gathered family and friends was that with the help of years of physical therapy I'd be able to eat, brush my teeth, and get dressed on my own.

The confusion, tension, and emotion in the hospital was swirling past the point of no return. People were exhausted. No one had slept or showered. Tears flooded the ward. The realization that I might never have a normal conversation with any of them again started to set in.

Then it happened.

One of the lead doctors walked into the waiting room with a grim look on his face. Everyone looked up from their phones and temporarily forgot about their petty beefs.

"I'm sorry," the doctor began in a solemn tone. "If you would like to say your last words to Lamar, I think you should start getting your thoughts together."

This is the absolute darkest moment of life.

Today is the day I'm going to die.

It's my time to fade into the ether. I, Lamar Odom, will merge with the infinite. I will see my mom again. I wonder if she will recognize me. Mildred will be there, too. My son. I will go into that sweet good night. I will go from the darkness to the light.

And my spirit wants to leave. But for some reason it can't. It's stuck. Something is holding on to it. Then I see what's keeping me earthbound: Destiny and Lamar Jr. I held them when they were babies. I wouldn't let them go. Now Destiny held me in the palm of her tiny hand. Lamar Jr. wouldn't let me go. Their voices echoed in chambers of my heart. Their love coursed through my veins. I was reborn.

I would not die that day.

A surge of life jolted through my body, nearly lifting me out of that hospital bed. I'm five feet in the air if I'm an inch. I want to scream but I can't.

I am closer to God in this moment than I've ever been.

I sit up in bed and furiously begin pulling all of the tubes from my body. I rip the neuron sensors off my forehead. A cry goes up from everyone in the waiting room. Khloé screams. Kylie is bawling. Alarms and bells go off. The doctors come sprinting down the hallways. They quickly ready shots. This is new territory for them. Panic and chaos hit the second floor like a tidal wave. My monitors are going haywire. Clipboards are flying all over the place.

People start to pray.

They have never seen a miracle before.

I open my eyes for the first time in forty-eight hours. From the darkness to the light.

This is the first day of the rest of my life.

This is not the final portrait of Lamar.

I'm not ready.

I've learned so many lessons in this life. I've failed just as much as I've succeeded. I fall down. I get up. Or God picks me up. Or my kids do. Not the final portrait, indeed.

We are born, we live, and we die. But I did not die that day. I will keep breathing. I will keep loving. And I will believe. Today, I will live.

29

I had survived, but I still needed to live. I was still an addict. After the hospital, my life was up and down and directionless. I had recovered physically, more or less, but I was as vulnerable as I had ever been.

So, in November 2016, Greg organized an intervention in the two-bedroom apartment that I lived in just off Ventura Boulevard in the Valley. Greg, Al Harris, Liza, Destiny, and Lamar Jr. were there. I came home after hanging out with friends. I did not expect this shit. I was caught off guard and didn't know how to react. I saw Destiny and Lamar Jr. I was shocked.

"What are y'all doing in my apartment?" I asked.

"Sit down, bro," Greg said.

I resisted.

"No, you need to sit down, Lamar," said Al Harris, my lifelong friend. "This is real. We have to talk."

The room got quiet. My entire family was here. All of my friends. From Queens. From Miami. From my Lakers days. There were nearly a dozen people. I was nervous, scared, and defensive. I was being ambushed and I knew why. They wanted to save me.

I saw Destiny. She was crying already. I broke down. Her beautiful face was the only thing stronger than the pull of drugs.

Her love was stronger than addiction.

"There is nothing to lie about, bro," said Greg. "You know, and we need to fix it. Your children are here. It's now or never."

I looked at Destiny. My beautiful baby girl. Born in the summer of my eighteenth year. She didn't choose her name or her destiny. I gave both to her. Tears streamed down her face. I broke. I died in that moment.

"Are you okay, Daddy?" she said.

My seventeen-year-old baby girl. I heard the words. It was like a rocket shot me through a wall. There was an explosion of drywall and realization. Because my firstborn had tears running down her face.

I remembered when I was first with Liza. It was a cold December day. We were kids. I told her everything would be okay. She got pregnant. Our lives changed from that day forward.

Then LJ spoke.

"I hate this," said Lamar Jr. "I hate being scared. I hate not knowing if you're going to call me. I hate not knowing when I wake up if you're going to be alive. I'm scared."

That really fucking scared me.

The room stopped, as did my heart. LJ is an incredibly quiet child. I had never heard him speak like this. He was fourteen years old, a beautiful, strong, independent boy.

Unlike his father, who was a coward. Scared of mirrors, lest he see what he'd become. I didn't want LJ to look at me. I saw myself in LJ. I saw my father in me. There was no way LJ saw himself in me. But I was still his dad. But I was also sick. My son was stronger than me.

That hurt me worst of all. Grown men were crying. No one could talk. LJ stared at me. Liza buried her face in her hands.

I had met her in homeroom at Christ the King when I was the same age as my son was now. I was young and innocent. I wasn't an addict. I wasn't famous or rich. I took the bus to get to school. I thought she was pretty.

They laid it out for me.

"Rehab or we ain't fucking with you," said Greg.

After it was over, I went into the back room. Destiny and LJ followed. I told them that I loved them.

"Daddy, I don't want see you like this," said Destiny.

My heart died. My baby girl. The most beautiful accomplishment of my life had told me that she wanted me to live. I broke down.

Then Greg came in.

"It's this or nothing," he said. "We gotta do rehab."

"Let me think about it," I said.

Even after seeing my devastated children, I didn't go to rehab right away. The intervention didn't work. Liza and the kids went back home to New York. Greg continued with his life. I went back to what I was doing the moment before I walked in on them in my apartment. A few days later, Greg got a phone call.

It was Bunim/Murray Productions, which produced *Keeping Up with the Kardashians* and *Khloé & Lamar*. They wanted to do another show, titled *Rebound*. It would be about my life after death and how I would make it back. They were ready to cut a $200,000 check up front. Greg came over to my house and dropped the news.

"The money is there," said Greg. "But there's one condition."

"What's that?" I asked.

"I don't want to have anything to do with you unless you go to rehab. Thirty days. It has to be now."

But rehab is expensive. This discreet facility in San Diego was going to cost $100,000. Sobriety ain't cheap. To pay for it, a show called *The Doctors* agreed to cover the cost in exchange for an exclusive interview before and after I left rehab. They shot the "before" interview at Greg's house. The next day, Greg drove me to Casa Palmera in San Diego. I checked in for alcohol, drug, and sex addiction. It's a beautiful, expansive campus where they pamper you and treat you like royalty. But you're not allowed to have a cell phone, even though I was able to hook up a burner phone so I could keep in contact with people. A few days after I checked in, there was a friends and family day. Greg, Liza, Destiny, and Lamar Jr. all showed up.

It was going well and everyone was happy that I was getting the help I needed. The doctors and specialists discussed my history and explained how my addictions manifested and stemmed from my need to self-medicate. I spent Christmas and New Year's there. I did the full thirty days, and then Greg picked me up. I felt healthy and refreshed in a way I'd never felt before. I thought then that I was gonna be all right. When I got in the car, Greg handed me $50,000 in cash as part of the payment from Bunim/Murray Productions—$50K feels heavy in your hands. Then we got the hell out of there.

A few days later, my friends organized a welcome home party for me at The Lobster, my favorite restaurant in Santa Monica. Everyone was there. Luke Walton. My old teammate Brian Shaw. Keyon Dooling. People from Queens. Greg and his wife. It was an amazing night and I felt truly loved.

THE LAST CHAPTER

Joseph. That name. That is my middle name. That was my father's name. He got it from his father. It is the most important thing I have. It informs who I have been and who I am. My father's son.

Joseph.

I am who I am. I cannot undo who I am. I am ultimately thankful for who I am.

I look at my life now.

I can see the future. I can see where I've been. I can see the people I love.

Greg is still married, with four kids. He's doing well. I remember when I first met him in a gym in Queens. We became teammates and best friends.

Sonny and Pam Vaccaro are still together. They live in Malibu. He spends his days fighting the NCAA. He still cooks every night. Ask him about his pasta Bolognese.

Khloé and her boyfriend, NBA star Tristan Thompson, welcomed their first child into the world. I am happy for them. She will be an amazing mother.

Liza lives in New York with Destiny and Lamar Jr. She has been my rock through it all. I still remember her pretty face from homeroom freshman year.

Destiny will be twenty-one soon. She wants to be a dancer.

Lamar Jr. is six feet three. He is quiet, polite, and respectful. He has none of his father's habits.

Gary Charles lives with his family in Long Island. He is still involved with the Panthers and works in New York's financial district.

Taraji is the star of *Empire*, one of the best shows on television. She is still a perfect example of black womanhood.

Tavorris Bell lives in Atlanta, Georgia. He works at a publishing company. He often visits his seventeen-year-old daughter in Miami. I regularly bust his ass in NBA 2K.

Jerry DeGregorio, Poppa D, is an assistant coach with women's basketball at Clemson.

Aunt JaNean still lives at 131st and Linden. She's as feisty as ever. She's still Aunt JaNean.

Joseph, my father, lives in Brooklyn, not far from the Woodside Houses where he met my mother forty-one years ago. I talk to him once a week.

As for me, I'm still an addict. I still struggle. Some days I don't want to get out of bed. Some days I feel like the world and everything in it is mine. I still have my sense of humor. I can still see the bright side.

I'm hopeful. I'm determined. I am fierce. I am blessed. I am a force. I am humbled.

But mostly, I'm still figuring out who I am. I'm in a good place. I love the journey I'm on, and it's nowhere near done.

I will not go into the darkness. Ever again. I remember Grandma Mildred. I crave the light. I went from the darkness to the light. I died. And now I live. It is truly a gift. I still struggle. Pray for me because I will pray for you. If you see me, come up and say hello. Every person I meet is a light. Every smile, kind word, beautiful gesture is something that will keep me from the darkness.

I've never been truly able to express how I feel about the fans. You know what? Not fans. Just friends I've never met. I've been as low as a person can go. But you never let me fall. You kept me from the pit of despair. Your love saved my life even if I've never met you. Your spirit is with me. Thank you. Your love has been a light that has never gone out. These pages must show.

One day I will meet my mother again. I will tell her about my life, and I will ask her about hers. I will hold her as she once held me. I will tell her I tried to be kind to everyone. Just like she told me to be the last time I talked to her. I will tell her that Mookah did his best.

I will hug my mother and I will cry. I won't ask why. I will tell her that I kept our room clean. I was tall and handsome and polite. Just like she wanted her boy to be. I hope she still loves me. I will tell her that I love her. I will hug my mom.

But not yet.

I am thirty-nine.
This is where I was born.
This is where she died.
I can close my eyes and still see it.
I will die.
But I will not die today.
I will not go into that sweet good night.

Not yet.

I made it this far.
I have lived to tell.
I am Lamar Joseph Odom.
And I am alive.

ACKNOWLEDGMENTS

First, I would like to thank God for the opportunity to tell the story of my life. It has been an incredible journey filled with amazing people, as these pages will show. Thank you to one of the most loyal, trustworthy women to ever come into my life, the mother of my children, Liza Morales. You have been more than patient, forgiving, and understanding when it came to my wild ways. I didn't deserve your love, but you gave it to me nonetheless. My children Destiny Odom and Lamar Jr., whom I love unconditionally. They loved me despite my absence from their lives at times, and there's no love that I can give like the love I get from them.

I want to thank my mother, Cathy Mercer. Not a day goes by without me thinking about you. Each day I realize how much you gave me in such a short time. I wish you could see the man I am today. Your granddaughter, Destiny, looks more like you every day. I know you're in heaven holding Jayden's hand. My grandmother, your mother, Mildred Mercer, kept my spirit intact when you went away, and she will forever be a piece of my soul.

Thank you to Aunt JaNean, who is the last connection I have to my mother and grandmother.

There have been so many people who have helped shape my basketball experience over the last three decades, including Gary Charles, Jerry DeGregorio, Sonny Vaccaro, Jeff Schwartz, Rob Johnson, Tom Konchalski, and Jim Harrick.

Much love for the hundreds of teammates I got to call my brothers. Kobe Bryant, from whom I learned everything about competing and giving yourself to the game. I tried my best to keep that Mamba Mentality whenever we stepped on the floor together. You are my brother for life.

Pau Gasol, Dwyane Wade, Rasual Butler, Speedy Claxton, Ira Miller, Darius Miles, Quentin Richardson, Elton Brand, Ron Artest, and Tavorris Bell are some of the best brothers I've ever had.

I was fortunate enough to have great teachers in Phil Jackson, Pat Riley, and Alvin Gentry. They not only taught me what it means to be a well-rounded player but also what it means to be a man. Thank you to Jeanie Buss for her kindness and compassion.

To Khloé Kardashian, the love of my life. I wish I could have been a better man. Thank you to the entire Kardashian family for embracing me and giving me an incredible kind of love. I will always be "Lammy."

No man takes a journey by himself, and I've had some great people to accompany me along the way: James "Dollar" Gregory, Lara "Cake" Manoukian, Greg Nunn, Joseph Odom, Curt Smith, George "Boss" Revas, Ian Dominic, Alley Cat, and Big John.

Thank you all for being part of my journey.

ABOUT THE AUTHOR

LAMAR ODOM is a two-time NBA champion, former Sixth Man of the Year, and thirteen-year NBA veteran. He was a regular cast member on *E!*'s worldwide sensation *Keeping Up with the Kardashians*, the highest-rated reality show in history. He also starred in the popular spin-off *Khloé & Lamar*, which documented one of the most famous marriages in recent Hollywood memory. He calls Queens home but lives in Los Angeles.

CHRIS PALMER is a longtime sportswriter who covered the National Basketball Association for twenty years for *ESPN The Magazine* and all of ESPN's digital platforms. He is currently a contributor for ESPN's The Undefeated, Spectrum SportsNet, as well as various other outlets. He's the author/contributor of six books, including *Wide Open*, the *New York Times* bestselling autobiography of Supercross champion Jeremy McGrath. He lives in Los Angeles.